CRAVINGS

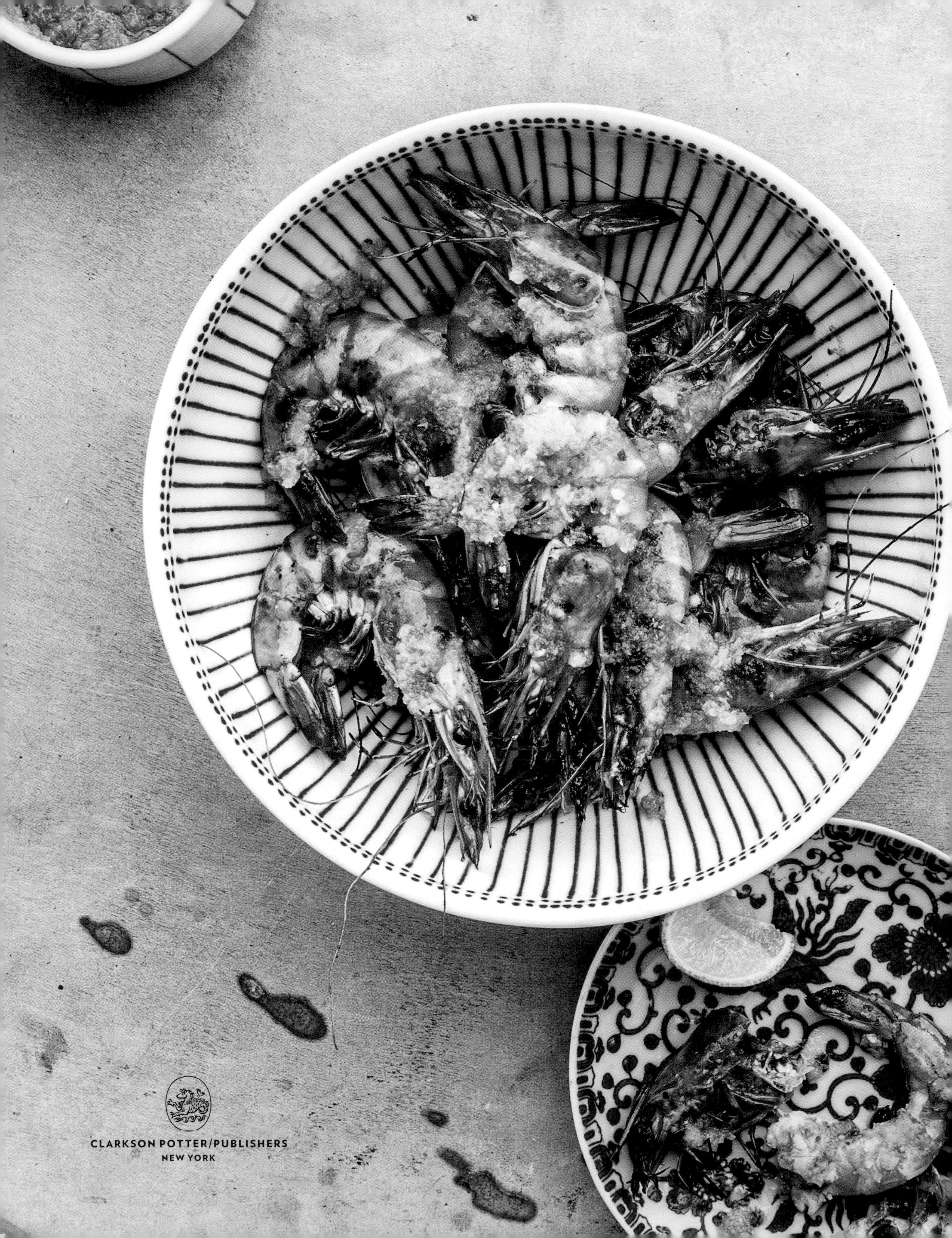

CLARKSON POTTER/PUBLISHERS
NEW YORK

RECIPES FOR ALL THE FOOD
YOU *WANT* TO EAT

CRAVINGS

Chrissy Teigen

with ADEENA SUSSMAN

Published in the United States by Clarkson Potter/Publishers, an imprint of the Crown Publishing Group, a division of Penguin Random House LLC, New York.
www.crownpublishing.com
www.clarksonpotter.com

Library of Congress Cataloging-in-Publication Data
Teigen, Chrissy, author. | Pick, Aubrie, photographer.
Cravings / Chrissy Teigen; photographs by Aubrie Pick.
First edition. | New York: Clarkson Potter/Publishers, [2016] | Includes index.
LCCN 2015034460 | ISBN 9781101903919 (hardcover) | ISBN 9781101903926 (ebook)
LCSH: Cooking. | LCGFT: Cookbooks.
LCC TX714 .T43 2016 | 641.5—dc23 LC record available at lccn.loc.gov/2015034460

ISBN 978-1-101-90391-9
Ebook ISBN 978-1-101-90392-6

Printed in the United States of America

Book design by Laura Palese
Cover design by Lemonade NY
Cover photographs by Aubrie Pick
Cover hand lettering by Laura Palese

10 9 8 7 6 5 4 3 2 1

First Edition

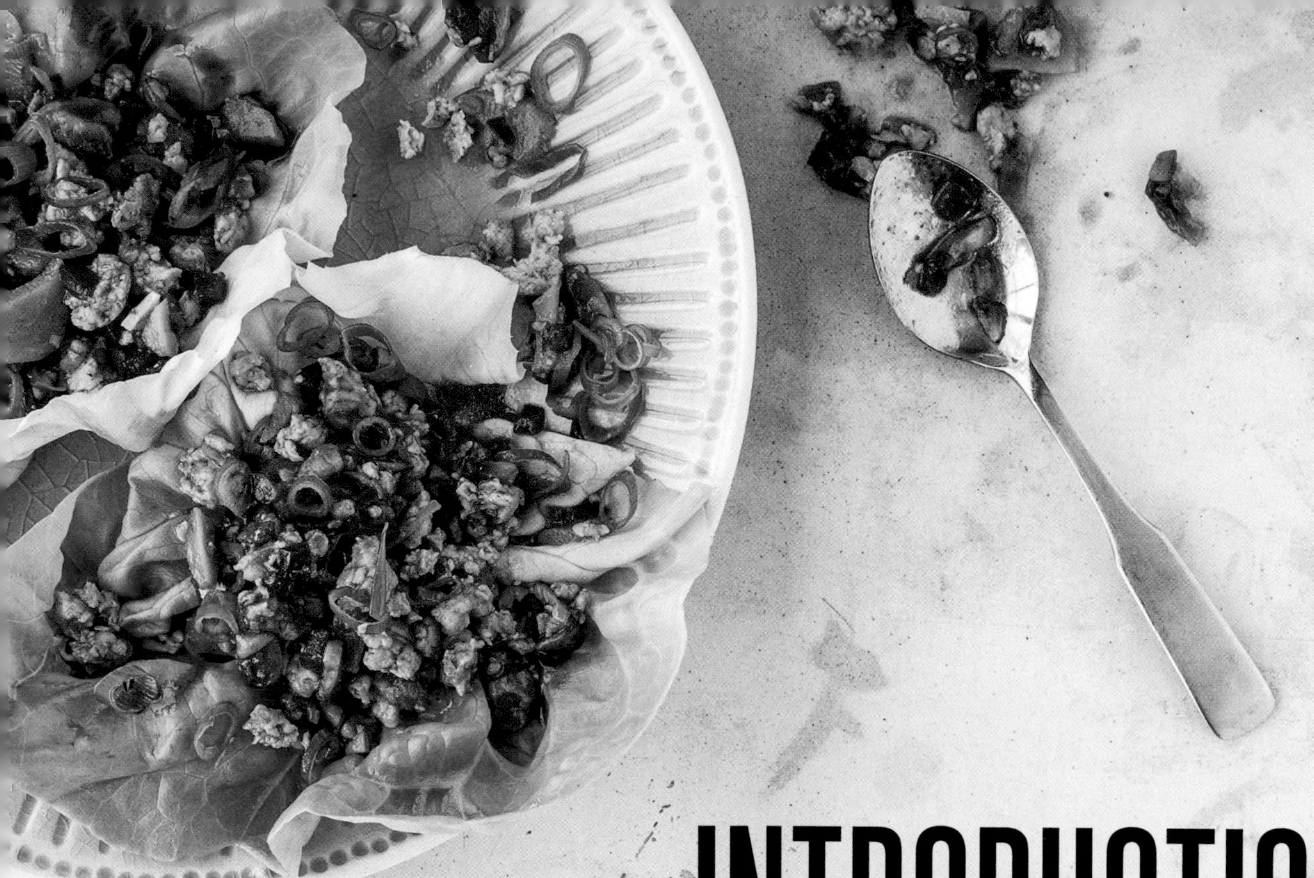

INTRODUCTION

I know, I know. A cookbook from me? The girl who had two fast-food Twitter accounts fighting for her affection in what was the oddest, greasiest exchange she had ever witnessed? The one whose visits to **Waffle House** and whose messed-up miscommunications with the Postmates dinner delivery guys make it to the Internet sometimes? The girl who actually celebrated Thanksgiving at **Taco Bell** headquarters among her closest friends she had never met? Yep. I am doing it. ***And doing it.*** (And doing it well.)

SO. THIS BOOK. My Thai mom is ESL, but I am FSL: Food has been my second language since I was a tiny little brat. A lot of kids wear superhero costumes, princess costumes. I used to fall asleep, so happy, wearing my little chef's hat or mom's chile pepper apron with oven mitts on. (Don't sleep in oven mitts you cooked in all day because ants will make you their bitch. See, you're learning something already!) I spent my childhood in the kitchen following around Thai Mom, who pretty much made everything from scratch, using tools none of my other friends had in their homes. I remember sitting cross-legged on the kitchen counter, an annoying trait I still possess, buttering piles and piles of crackers for dad's chicken soup, ripping up bacon for mom's scalloped potatoes. I remember, when my friends were over, plugging my nose and *pretending* to hate the exotic fish sauce my mom was using. I remember debating the finer points of flaky pastry with my chicken-pot-pie-obsessed American dad. I remember the divine mix of Thai food, TV dinners, and hearty, homemade goodness that have shaped this palate of mine to this day. I remember all this but I still google my husband's birthday. Thank god he's famous.

The kitchen is a place I know well. It's my favorite room wherever I am living, and it has to be completely open and social. Our kitchen has seen way more activity than our hot tub *or* sex dungeon. The kitchen is the heart of any home. And my heart is in the kitchen.

But whether for business or pleasure, I am almost always on a plane. Same with John. It's amazing—we've been to so many beautiful places around the world. We've eaten every sort of meal, at the finest French Michelin-star restaurants, BBQs in Texas, and street markets in the Thai village my mom grew up in. When I'm not traveling, though, I am basically a world-class shut-in.

When I am home, I am *home*, people, and if it wasn't for the fact that John wants genuine date-nights out with me, I would probably never. Ever. Leave. (Why he doesn't consider watching me watch *Real Housewives* a date-night, I will never understand.)

Which brings us to cooking. I am not lying when I tell you I can hang out in the kitchen for twelve hours straight without stopping. Just ask my live-in mom, who you might know as Pepper Thai (or, to be exact, @PepperThai2, which is her name because she doesn't remember the password to @PepperThai *or* @PepperThai1 so be on the lookout for @PepperThai3 by the time this thing comes out). Or ask all the friends who I make come over instead of going to their house UNLESS they give in to my demands of my bringing over some sort of small feast. When I am cooking, I am in the moment. I'm very slowwww, rereading recipes, sipping wine, munching, sipping vodka, more munching. I really get into the dish I am making. I relax. My day job may be exhausting, but cooking is my peace. My dream is to have a big family with lots of grandkids. And we'll get together every Sunday for a hearty dinner at our house, and we'll all live in flavorful bliss, happily ever after. (Or they could become vegans. *Oh my god, they could become vegans.*)

I started posting pictures of my meals on social media, and I could not believe the response. A few classy blokes asked for more TITTTAYYYYYY, but most of you are awesome. I'd post a picture of a dish (usually with some story of how I messed it up but it was delish anyway), and lots of you would tweet me back, ask me for a recipe, give me some tips, or just plain ol' get excited to get in the kitchen yourselves. We would have our #DrunkDinnerParties, posting pics of our successes and failures. And I started a little food blog called *So Delushious*. It's been amazing to share my love of food with you. I feel like I should pay you for the overwhelming joy it gives me when people tell me that something I posted got them excited to cook something for themselves.

So of course I had to write a cookbook, and of course I had to give you my best. I cooked and cooked with my cowriter, Adeena, until everything tasted

just how I wanted it—and then I cooked it again. And again for John. And again for friends. And AGAIN for the finicky eaters who don't like much of anything. Once we got those people excited, we knew we had the perfect cookbook. When it came to creating these recipes, I wanted this to be as simple as possible without skimping on the flavor. Cooking can be intimidating to a lot of people, and I want you to know you really can make a great meal without having gone to Le Cordon Bleu. I want the recipes to work every time, and without a jillion ingredients you have to go to twelve stores for. And I want them to taste UNFORGETTABLE. Like go-to-sleep-grinning because what you made was just so painfully, achingly incredible!

I know how I like my food. I like it spicy, salty, sticky, crunchy, juicy, oozy—basically any dish you know and love, jacked up to a bordering-on-socially-unacceptable amount of flavor. Let's face it, I do have to make every bite count, so if I'm gonna drag that fork to my mouth hole, it better taste crazy delicious. And I can promise you that everything in this book does.

If you're expecting a model to write a cookbook full of diet recipes for you to perfect your bikini bod, I think you'll be a little surprised here. These are recipes we love to indulge in with family and friends. Some more hearty than others, some even more hearty than the hearty ones. But every single recipe is something we love. Look, I don't want to be one of those dead-inside laughing-with-a-salad chicks, and I don't want to seem like one of those annoying "I can eat anything I want anytime" chicks. It's just that I wanted to be honest in this book about the kinds of food I love, the kinds of food I *crave*. I just have to find ways to make those cravings work with my day job (e.g., sometimes with a well-timed "f*ck it").

I've always loved cookbooks (I have hundreds) but what I haven't loved is having to flip through tons of different ones to find the stuff I like to make and eat. So when I decided to make one of my own I wanted it to be a bible you could flip open and use for every meal. Perfect eggs? Check. Soupmaster classics and the best salads ever? Yup. Dinner for a couple or a small group of friends? Totally. Snacks for football Sundays? Yes, indeed. They're all here—except dessert. I mean, I will go to an Italian restaurant and order another pasta while everyone else is enjoying their panna cotta. Also it is well documented how badly I suck at baking. So you'll have to Fudgie-the-Whale-it for dessert. Sorry!

So start flipping through, and start cooking! Nothing would make me happier than to know that this book has helped make your life a little bit more flavorful and interesting. I'm sure I'll be hearing from every single one of you really soon, so I'll begin clearing out my in-box . . . as soon as I clear my plate.

XOXOXO
Chrissy

BEFORE YOU START COOKING

Maybe you've never cooked a meal in your life, or maybe you are Chef Chefly McCheffington. Either way, here are some things to keep in mind while cooking these recipes. They're not rules, really, but little guidelines and tips to help you with the recipes in this book. And there are some things here that I always wished other people would tell me when I was starting. You're welcome!

SALT
Diamond (Crystal) Is Forever

Unless I specify otherwise, I only use Diamond Crystal brand kosher salt—it's like gold to me, and easy to pinch with your fingers. I love my food with plenty of salt, but Diamond Crystal is less "salty" than other kosher salts, so it's easier to control. It's the standard for everything I cook—if you're using Morton's, *decrease* the salt measurements in these recipes by one third to account for its more concentrated saltiness. Or start low and taste as you cook, adding more salt gradually along the way until it tastes great to you.

PEPPER

Pretty much everything I make has a generous amount of pepper from a pepper grinder. Freshly ground pepper has incredible flavor compared to the stale, powdery pepper you get in the jar, and is actually less sneezy. If you're not fresh-grinding, you might want to reduce the pepper quantities a bit.

HOT SAWCE

I am a chile fiend. Always have the following in the house if you can: Sriracha (also known as "Teigen's ketchup"; my bad bitch Cholula hot sauce; sambal oelek (see page 87); cayenne pepper; red pepper flakes; and fresh and dried Thai bird chiles. That way, if the spice level I call for in any recipe isn't enough for you (which would impress me), you can add as little or as much as you like.

PARMESAN

You can use regular old Parmesan cheese in these recipes, but I always call for the O.G.: Parmigiano-Reggiano. The cool thing about Parmigiano-Reggiano is that (a) it comes from Italy, (b) it basically makes anything it touches taste amazing, and (c) it keeps forever in the fridge. This is aged cheese, and it has these tiny little crunchy crystals inside (taste a little chunk and you'll see for yourself). It's pricey—the older it is (usually 12, 18, or 24 months) the more expensive. To store, wrap in special cheese-wrapping paper, or wrap loosely in plastic wrap so it can breathe a little. Pro tip: Don't throw away the inedible hard rind; throw it into a minestrone soup or any clear brothy soup—it will deepen the soup's flavor—then take it out before serving.

When I say "grated Parm," I pretty much am always talking about grating it on a Microplane grater. You can get one anywhere, and it makes the lightest, most feathery shavings. When I call for shredded or grated cheddar or mozzarella, though, use the large holes on a box grater. And I don't hate on the pregrated stuff in the store. I mean, it's cheese.

TOASTING NUTS

I pretty much always toast my nuts before using them. (Wait, are you laughing? There are going to be *actual* jokes in this book.) Toasting brings out the flavor locked inside these little babies. To do it, put the nuts in a dry skillet and heat over medium heat, shaking pretty often, until the nuts are toasty and fragrant, anywhere from 5 to 8 minutes, depending on the kind of nut. When they're hot and shiny and just a little darker, they're done. Pour them onto a plate right away or else they'll burn.

BASIC KNIFE CUTS *(knowing these does not make you basic)*

Cubed is for when you want big squares, like ¾ to 1 inch. Diced is smaller, like ½ inch. Chopped is chopped up into little bits. And minced is when you just chop and chop while you're watching TV until everything is really tiny or, in the case of finely minced garlic, when you use a garlic press. (Also, JK, don't chop and watch TV at the same time. I love your fingers the way they are.)

And then there's our girlfriend Julienne. Julienne is French for fancy-looking thin strips. You can accomplish this by cutting whatever you want into really thin sheets, stacking them, and then cutting the stacks into thin strips. Or you can go to the store and buy a "julienne peeler," which does all this for you and works great on things like carrots, cucumbers, and green papayas.

Some BASIC MEASUREMENTS

1 stick butter	=	8 tablespoons or 4 ounces or ½ cup or ¼ pound *(How can there be this many ways to say the same thing?)*
1 small onion	=	1 cup diced
1 medium onion	=	1½ cups diced
1 large onion	=	2 cups diced
3 teaspoons	=	1 tablespoon
2 tablespoons	=	1 liquid ounce
8 ounces	=	1 cup
2 cups	=	1 pint
4 cups	=	1 quart
16 cups	=	1 gallon
For weight, 16 ounces	=	1 pound

BREAKFAST ALL DAY

// *Opposite:* Cajun Catfish with Over-Easy Eggs (PAGE 35)

SERVES 4 TO 6

PREP TIME: 5 minutes **TOTAL TIME:** 20 minutes

CHEESY CHEESELESS SCRAMBLED EGGS WITH BURST CHERRY TOMATOES

I consume eggs more than any human should: hard-boiled, rolled in salt and pepper, dipped into Sriracha, little poachies with garlic toast soldiers, over-easy with a gooey wet yolk I mop up with avocado and turkey bacon (I am the only human that admits to loving rubbery, processed turkey bacon). But these . . . these scrambled eggs are my special babies.

This takes a bit of time, but I promise you: They're called my Cheesy Cheeseless eggs for a reason. They come out so rich and dense and creamy, and it's all just in the technique (well, technique and a little heavy cream). So pull a barstool up to the stove and slowly stir your little heart out while watching *Housewives*. (I mean, I don't watch that trash. . . . I mean, who cares about Dorinda and Vicki and Tamra and her gym and Briana's baby and Kenya being Gone-with-the-Wind fabulous and Kim and her aggro dog? I've never seen an episode in my life.)

for the **EGGS**

- **12 really good-quality eggs (the ones with the really yellow yolks)**
- **½ cup heavy cream**
- **1 teaspoon kosher salt, plus more to taste**
- **¼ teaspoon freshly ground black pepper**
- **3 tablespoons olive oil**
- **3 tablespoons butter**

for the **BURST CHERRY TOMATOES**

- **2 tablespoons olive oil**
- **3 cups cherry tomatoes (about 1 pound)**
- **½ teaspoon kosher salt**
- **¼ teaspoon freshly ground black pepper**

- **¼ cup thinly sliced chives (optional)**
- **Garlic-Roasted Bacon (optional; recipe follows)**

MAKE THE EGGS: In a bowl, whisk the eggs, cream, salt, and pepper until they look like melted ice cream.

In a large nonstick skillet, heat the oil and butter over low heat until the butter is melted but not super hot. You will get the urge to bump up the heat—do not do it!!! Add the eggs and cook, stirring. This will test your patience and any tendencies toward ADHD. Cook, stirring incessantly, until the eggs are custardy and form small curds, 12 to 14 minutes. Remove from the heat.

MAKE THE TOMATOES: During the last 10 minutes of egg-cookin' time, heat a large cast-iron or other heavy skillet over medium-high heat until really hot (it should be hard to get your hand close to the skillet). Add the oil and swirl it around, then add the tomatoes and sprinkle with the salt and pepper. Let the tomatoes cook, tossing every couple of minutes, until they're blistered and kind of shriveled, 5 to 6 minutes total.

Serve the eggs hot with the chives on top, if using, the tomatoes, and the bacon, if desired. Season with more salt and pepper.

garlic-roasted bacon

SERVES 3 TO 6

PREP TIME: 3 minutes
TOTAL TIME: 20 minutes

The most exciting things for me to write about are the little things, the tricks you learn and wonder, "Why was I doing it any other way before?" The Cheesy Cheeseless Eggs are like that. And if you have the time, this is the way to do bacon. No more weirdo, half-cooked curls, no more oil splatters destroying your spray tan. And the smell. Oh my god, the *smell of roasted bacon*. One time our neighbors (OK, actually *our* house) had some sewage issues and I threw some bacon in the oven just to get through the day. It worked. Follow me on Twitter for more #sewagetips.

12 slices thick-cut bacon
3 cloves garlic, chopped

Preheat the oven to 375°F.

Lay the bacon out on a rimmed baking sheet so the slices don't overlap. Sprinkle the garlic all over the bacon. Roast until crisp, 12 to 15 minutes. (Even if you don't use the garlic, this is still the best way to cook bacon.)

SERVES 4

PREP TIME: 5 minutes **TOTAL TIME:** 25 minutes

DUTCH BABY PANCAKE

- **1 cup all-purpose flour, sifted**
- **4 large eggs**
- **1 cup whole milk, at room temperature**
- **½ teaspoon kosher salt**
- **4 tablespoons (½ stick) butter, melted, plus softened butter for serving**
- **Pancake syrup (or, more specifically, Mrs. Butterworth's)**
- **Powdered sugar, for dusting**

. . . or is it German? Or Swedish? Well, I totally get why all these countries are trying to claim this gem of a breakfast sweet. My dad used to make these when I was growing up, before I realized I couldn't jump-start my day by consuming 2,000 calories. Basically it's a fluffy dough bucket—a dish that, when finished, acts as a vessel to transport buttery syrup and powdered sugar into your mouth hole. They puff up ever-so-perfectly and one bite will change your life. Add some lemon zest if you're feeling Paltrow-y or eat it right out of the pan if you're in more of a Teigen kind of mood.

Preheat the oven to 475°F.

In a blender, combine the flour, eggs, milk, salt, and 2 tablespoons of the melted butter and blend until smooth with no lumps, 20 to 30 seconds.

In a 10-inch cast-iron skillet, heat the remaining 2 tablespoons melted butter over high heat until foamy. Add the batter and immediately put the skillet in the oven. Bake until the outside of the pancake is puffed and a deep golden color (it will puff up in a bit of a crazy, disorganized way, so don't worry), 17 to 18 minutes.

Remove from the oven, slather with softened butter, and cut into quarters. Pour syrup over the pancake slices and dust with powdered sugar.

SERVES 4

PREP TIME: 30 minutes **TOTAL TIME:** 1 hour 30 minutes

CRAB CAKES BENEDICT WITH AVOCADO

"How can I make this lower in carbs and more delicious?" is what I ask when starting lots of my recipes. By replacing the traditional English muffin in Eggs Benedict with crabmeat, I can sleep knowing I have completed my goal. And is there anything worse than a bready crab cake? I hate fillers. (Well, food fillers; I'm all for the face ones, even if my face kind of needs the opposite.) Anyhoo . . . that running yolk seeping into your greens with the lumpy crab and red pepper sauce? The ultimate.

for the **FAKE HOLLANDAISE**

- ½ cup mayonnaise
- ¼ cup Sriracha
- 1 teaspoon minced garlic
- ¼ teaspoon kosher salt

for the **CRAB CAKES**

- 1 large egg
- 2 tablespoons mayonnaise
- 1½ teaspoons Dijon mustard
- 1 teaspoon Sriracha
- 1 teaspoon Worcestershire sauce
- ½ teaspoon kosher salt
- ½ teaspoon freshly ground black pepper
- 2 tablespoons minced chives
- ¾ pound lump crabmeat, picked over
- ⅓ cup fine fresh bread crumbs
- ½ cup canola oil

for the **EGGS**

- 2 cups baby arugula
- 1 small avocado, sliced
- ½ teaspoon distilled white vinegar or lemon juice
- 4 eggs
- Freshly ground black pepper

MAKE THE FAKE HOLLANDAISE: In a bowl, stir together the mayonnaise, Sriracha, garlic, and salt until combined. Refrigerate until ready to use.

MAKE THE CRAB CAKES: In a bowl, whisk together the egg, mayo, mustard, Sriracha, Worcestershire, salt, pepper, and chives. Add the crabmeat and bread crumbs and gently fold, trying not to break up the crab. (It's just a little bit of bread crumb to hold the cakes together, not a filler!) Form into 4 crab cakes, arrange them on a plate, cover, and refrigerate for 1 hour.

In a large skillet, heat the oil over medium-high heat. When the oil is shimmering-hot, gently lay the crab cakes in the oil and fry until golden on the underside, 4 minutes. Gently flip and fry an additional 4 minutes. Drain on paper towels and cover with foil to keep warm.

POACH THE EGGS: Bring a large skillet of water to a simmer over high heat.

Divide the arugula and avocado among 4 plates and top each plate with a crab cake. Cover with foil to keep warm.

Add the vinegar to the simmering water. Crack the eggs into individual small bowls and slip the eggs into the simmering water, remove the pan from the heat, cover, and let cook until the whites are solid, 3 to 4 minutes.

Using a slotted spoon, drain the eggs from the water and top each crab cake with an egg. Spoon some fake hollandaise sauce over each egg, season with pepper, and serve right away.

peeling/ pitting an avocado

Use a sharp chef's knife to cut into the avocado lengthwise, hitting the pit. Then roll the avocado along the blade to make a complete 360-degree cut. Gently twist one side of the avocado away from the other so you have two halves. Whack the pit with the heel of the knife and lift out the pit (you may have to jiggle it a little). Slip a large spoon between the flesh and peel and scoop out the avocado half.

LE CREUSET

SERVES 2

PREP TIME: 5 minutes **TOTAL TIME:** 10 minutes

CREAMY PARMESAN SKILLET EGGS

- **1 cup finely grated Parmigiano-Reggiano cheese**
- **½ cup heavy cream**
- **1 teaspoon chopped fresh thyme, plus more for garnish**
- **¼ teaspoon kosher salt, plus more to taste**
- **½ teaspoon freshly ground black pepper, plus more to taste**
- **2 tablespoons butter**
- **4 eggs**

These eggs are my personal go-to for brunches. (Can we just call brunch what it is? It's morning alcohol. We're boozing in the morning.) The cream in the pan makes these eggs easy to control without overcooking for all your bourgie, brunch-loving friends! Plus, I love cream's flavor punch. Combined with the cheese, it caramelizes into a sort of crust under the eggs. What's the point of a bite unless it's one of the best possible?

In a medium bowl, whisk together the Parm, cream, thyme, salt, and pepper.

In each of two 6-inch skillets, heat 1 tablespoon of the butter over medium-high heat. Divide the cream mixture between the two skillets and cook until the mixture is bubbling all the way through, 1 to 2 minutes. Crack 2 eggs into each skillet and cook until the egg whites are set but yolks are runny, 2 to 3 minutes. Season with salt and pepper to taste and garnish with some thyme.

(You can also do this in one large skillet, but it's cuter in small ones.)

SERVES 3 TO 6

PREP TIME: 10 minutes **TOTAL TIME:** 20 minutes

SPICY TOMATO SKILLET EGGS
WITH PROSCIUTTO

4 cups Perfect Tomato Sauce (page 82)
1 teaspoon red pepper flakes, or more to taste
6 eggs
Kosher salt
8 thin slices prosciutto (3 ounces)
2 tablespoons extra-virgin olive oil
1 tablespoon chopped fresh oregano
Buttered toast, for dipping

I am the busiest lazy person on the planet. I don't even know how it's possible to be both, but oh, I manage. I also regret every plan I've ever made. Did I invite you over for brunch? I'm dreading it. But luckily, I ALWAYS have the ingredients for this divine, painfully simple crowd-pleaser. Sopping up the eggy tomato sauce with focaccia *almost* makes me not regret inviting someone into my home/getting out of bed.

(Oh, and by the way, if I'm calling you, be a doll and please don't. Ever. Answer. Send me to voicemail. It is the greatest gift.)

In a heavy 12-inch skillet, combine the tomato sauce and red pepper flakes and cook over medium-high heat until the sauce is bubbling. Form 6 wells in the sauce and crack an egg into each well. Reduce the heat to medium, season the eggs with salt, and cook until the whites are set but the yolks are runny, 8 to 9 minutes. Midway through the cooking, tear the prosciutto and form it into little bundles, then tuck them into the sauce all around the pan. Drizzle everything with the olive oil, garnish with the oregano, and serve with toast.

MAKES 4 SANDWICHES

PREP TIME: 10 minutes **TOTAL TIME:** 25 minutes

JOHN'S BREAKFAST SANDWICHES

for the **SAUSAGE PATTIES**

- ½ pound ground pork
- ¼ cup finely minced onion
- 1 tablespoon light brown sugar
- 1 tablespoon minced garlic (about 2 cloves)
- 1 tablespoon vegetable oil, plus more for frying
- 1½ teaspoons ground sage
- 1½ teaspoons red pepper flakes
- 1½ teaspoons kosher salt
- ½ teaspoon freshly ground black pepper

for the **SANDWICHES**

- 4 English muffins
- 2 tablespoons butter
- Kosher salt and freshly ground black pepper (optional)
- 8 regular or 4 thick slices American cheese
- 4 eggs, cooked sunny-side up
- Sriracha

As told by the Legend himself: "The first song I wrote directly inspired by Chrissy was a song called 'Good Morning,' from my album *Evolver*. That song is not about making her a breakfast sandwich. It's about making . . . something else. But she LOVES my breakfast sandwich. And I LOVE good mornings. So the a.m. is a wonderful time in our house. Enjoy!"

MAKE THE SAUSAGE PATTIES: In a large bowl, mix the pork, onion, brown sugar, garlic, vegetable oil, sage, red pepper flakes, salt, and pepper with your hands until uniform (don't, like, mash it or overmix it—just until it's all nicely mixed together). Form into four 4-inch round patties.

Coat a cast-iron skillet with oil and heat over medium-high heat. Add the sausage patties and fry until browned and cooked through, about 4 minutes per side (8 minutes total). Transfer to a platter and cover to keep warm.

ASSEMBLE THE SANDWICHES: Split and toast the English muffins, then butter them. Season with a pinch of salt and pepper if you'd like. Arrange 1 thick or 2 regular slices of cheese on 4 of the muffin halves. Top each with a sausage patty and an egg. Squirt some Sriracha on top of the eggs and top with the remaining muffin halves.

PEANUTS

FBI STING NAILS HULK
IN RACIST RANTS
ENQUIRER
Whitney
MURDER
FINGERPRINT
NAILS THE
KILLER!
Boyfriend Nick Gordon's
Alibi DESTROYED —
What He's STILL HIDING
Terrified Words

SERVES 2

PREP TIME: 10 minutes **TOTAL TIME:** 25 minutes

CRISPY BACON HASH BROWNS

- 2 tablespoons vegetable oil
- 2 tablespoons butter, melted
- ¾ teaspoon kosher salt, plus more to taste
- 1 (8-ounce) potato (see Note)
- 2 slices bacon, minced
- ½ teaspoon freshly ground black pepper, plus more to taste

IHOP hash browns are one of my many trashy guilty pleasures. I will go to IHOP and consume two to three plates of their hash browns because I'm married and who cares. I love their golden brown, buttery crispiness, their tender little insides, but most of all I love that IHOP doesn't f*cking *call* them hash browns and then *serve* me HOME FRIES. THERE IS A DIFFERENCE, PEOPLE. I don't send anything back at restaurants, but I cannot help but open my rant hole and make a stink every time hash browns (shredded) get replaced by home fries (chunks). It's kiiiiiind of like pizza vs. ice cream, but if the hash browns were a pizza that was amazing and the home fries were ice cream that kinda sucks. Anyway. My hash browns have bacon in them. (See photograph, page 26.)

In a bowl, combine the oil, butter, and ¼ teaspoon of the salt and whisk to dissolve the salt.

Heat a medium cast-iron, nonstick, or plain-old whatever-you-have skillet over medium-high heat until your hand can feel strong heat if you hold it near the skillet, 4 to 5 minutes (don't add any of the butter mixture yet!).

Peel and grate the potato on the large holes of a box grater into a bowl. Toss it with the bacon, pepper, and the remaining ½ teaspoon salt. Dump the potato mixture into the skillet and spread it out into an 8-inch round, but don't pack it down too hard. Drizzle 3 tablespoons of the butter mixture evenly over the potatoes and cook, trying really hard not to move the potatoes, until the underside is golden and crispy, 4 to 5 minutes. Using a big spatula, try to flip the potatoes in one move, but forgive yourself immediately if you don't. Drizzle the rest of the butter mixture over the potatoes and cook until the underside is crisp, 4 to 5 minutes. Drain briefly on a paper towel, season with more salt and pepper if you want, and eat while hot and crispy!

note // Russet (Idaho) and waxier types both work well. Russets are crisper, waxier ones more buttery.

MAKES 9 BISCUITS AND 3 CUPS GRAVY

PREP TIME: 35 minutes **TOTAL TIME:** 1 hour

PULL-APART BUTTERMILK BISCUITS WITH SAUSAGE GRAVY

Somewhere out there lies the genius, no-f*cks-given human that stared up at the sky one night, wondering why it was socially unacceptable to eat gravy for breakfast. "Not anymore," he whispered. "Not anymore."

And thus biscuits and gravy were born and my life has never been the same. Have you ever pictured a pig lying in a bathtub full of syrup, drinking syrup?* Then pictured yourself dipping a sweet, maple biscuit into that bathtub and then putting that biscuit into your mouth? That's what this is.

* *I have pictured this.*

for the **SAUSAGE GRAVY**

- **¾ pound pork breakfast sausage, casings removed, crumbled**
- **4 tablespoons (½ stick) butter (see Note)**
- **¼ cup all-purpose flour (see Note)**
- **3 cups whole milk, plus more if necessary**
- **1½ teaspoons freshly ground black pepper**
- **1 teaspoon minced fresh sage**
- **1 teaspoon kosher salt**
- **½ teaspoon red pepper flakes**

for the **MAPLE CREAM**

- **6 tablespoons heavy cream**
- **3 tablespoons maple syrup**
- **1 teaspoon kosher salt**

note // If you like a runnier gravy, subtract 1 tablespoon each butter and flour.

MAKE THE SAUSAGE GRAVY: In a cast-iron skillet, cook the sausage over medium-high heat until browned and the fat is rendered, 4 to 5 minutes. Reduce the heat to medium-low, add the butter, stir to melt, then gradually sprinkle in the flour and cook until the sausage is coated and the flour is absorbed, about 2 minutes. Add the milk, return the heat to medium-high, and cook, stirring, until thick, about 10 minutes. (This requires patience, but stirring is sort of like meditation. Keep telling yourself this as you stir.) Add the black pepper, sage, salt, and red pepper flakes and cook, stirring, 2 minutes more. Remove from the heat and cover to keep warm.

MAKE THE MAPLE CREAM: In a bowl, combine the cream, maple syrup, and salt. Set aside.

MAKE THE BISCUITS: Preheat the oven to 425°F.

Put the butter in a small bowl, toss it with 2 tablespoons of the flour to coat, and put it in the freezer for 5 minutes.

In a food processor, combine the 3 cups flour, the baking powder, sugar, salt, and baking soda and pulse until incorporated. Pulse in the butter until some pea-size pieces remain, 15 to 20 pulses. Transfer the mixture to a big bowl and stir in the buttermilk until everything in the bowl is just moistened. (Don't overmix! Your bikkies will be tough, tough, tough if you do.)

// *recipe continues*

for the **BISCUITS**

- **1 stick (4 ounces) very cold unsalted butter, cut into ½-inch cubes (keep it in the fridge until you're ready to use it)**
- **3 cups plus 2 tablespoons all-purpose flour, plus more for kneading**
- **1 tablespoon baking powder**
- **1 teaspoon sugar**
- **1 teaspoon kosher salt**
- **½ teaspoon baking soda**
- **1½ cups buttermilk, shaken**

Transfer the dough to a floured surface, flour your hands, and knead the dough 3 to 4 times by folding down the top half of the dough, pressing on the pile with your palms, and turning the folded dough 90 degrees each time. Pat the dough into an 8-inch square 1 inch high. Cut it into 9 squares. Arrange the biscuits close together (like almost kissing) on a big baking sheet and brush with some of the maple cream.

Bake until golden, about 20 minutes, brushing with maple cream again 1 minute before removing.

Rewarm the sausage gravy over medium heat, adding a splash of milk to thin slightly, if desired. Serve with the biscuits and the remaining maple cream for dipping.

better biscuits

Fluffy biscuits start with *really* cold butter, which stays in solid pieces when you cut it into the dough. This means that when the biscuits bake, the butter melts, leaving little holes. More holes means more fluffiness!! So give your cold butter a short blast in the freezer to make it super extra cold. Also, make sure not to work the dough too much, which makes the biscuits tough and chewy. Mix everything *just enough* to incorporate and let it live.

SERVES 2

PREP TIME: 10 minutes **TOTAL TIME:** 25 minutes

CAJUN CATFISH
WITH OVER-EASY EGGS

for the **CAJUN SEASONING**

- 1 tablespoon minced garlic (about 2 cloves)
- 2 teaspoons paprika
- 1½ teaspoons dried thyme
- 1 teaspoon kosher salt, plus more for seasoning
- ½ teaspoon cayenne pepper, plus more for seasoning
- ½ teaspoon Tabasco sauce

for the **FISH AND EGGS**

- 4 tablespoons olive oil
- 2 (6-ounce) catfish fillets
- 1 tablespoon butter, plus more for toast
- 2 eggs
- 2 slices white bread
- Kosher salt and freshly ground black pepper
- ½ avocado, sliced

I am aware of how gross this sounds. Even I think it sounds gross. Every time I Instagram this personal favorite of mine, I get 60 percent "GOALLLLLLLS <3 <3 <3" (OK, I love it too, but come on, catfish should not be your goal. Just make some catfish. That's a really attainable goal you've set) and 40 percent "BARRRRRFFFFFZZZZ CATFISH." Why do you hate catfish so much? Is it because they are physically hideous bottom-feeders that consume purely water mud? God, you're so judgy. Errrrrmmmm . . . I am not really selling you this recipe well.

I love catfish. It's wonderfully hard to overcook unless you're really just an idiot, and its meat is naturally juicy, all while somehow being meaty and light at the same time. Plus, I would eat a fedora if it were covered in my Cajun seasoning. (See photograph, page 14.)

Preheat the oven to 425°F. Line a baking sheet with foil.

MAKE THE CAJUN SEASONING: In a small bowl, combine the garlic, paprika, thyme, salt, cayenne, and Tabasco.

MAKE THE FISH: Combine the seasoning mixture with 3 tablespoons of the olive oil and rub it all over the fish fillets. Place on the baking sheet and bake until cooked through but still juicy, about 12 minutes. Season with more salt and cayenne to taste.

MEANWHILE, FRY THE EGGS: Heat a large nonstick skillet over medium heat. Add the butter and remaining 1 tablespoon oil. After the butter foams, crack the eggs right into the skillet. Cook until the whites are set, 2 to 3 minutes. Flip the eggs and cook until the whites are just set and the yolks are still runny, 10 to 30 seconds, depending on how runny you like them.

Toast and butter the bread, slide one egg over each slice of bread, and season with salt and pepper. Serve with the catfish and avocado slices.

SERVES 8 TO 10

PREP TIME: 10 minutes **TOTAL TIME:** 1 hour

YELLOW CAKE BAKED OATMEAL

- 1 stick (4 ounces) butter, melted, plus softened butter for greasing the dish
- 5 cups whole milk
- 2 cups quick-cooking oats
- 2 cups yellow cake mix (from a box mix)
- 4 large eggs, beaten
- ¼ teaspoon kosher salt
- 1½ cups raspberries (about 6 ounces)
- 1 large or 2 small ripe peaches, sliced

That's right, buddy. Watching us come up with this recipe was like watching a group of stoners, except I am not into pot or weed or ganja or whatever it is called these days. I mean, I dip pizza bagels into Cholula butter and second-course it with Top Ramen salad *dead sober.* Can you imagine what weed does to me? Actually, maybe I go full opposite and am like, "Duuddddddde let's go get a saladdddddd." That would be awesome. This . . . tastes exactly how it sounds. Like heaven.

Preheat the oven to 350°F. Grease a 10 × 12-inch baking dish with butter.

In a large microwave-safe bowl, combine the milk and oats and microwave on high, stopping once to stir, 5 to 6 minutes. Let the oatmeal sit on the counter to thicken for 10 minutes, but not longer if possible because you want the oatmeal to finish doing its thing in the oven.

Stir the cake mix into the cooked oatmeal until smooth, then mix in the eggs, melted butter, and salt.

Transfer the batter to the prepared baking dish, then scatter the berries and peaches on top. Bake until the center is just set and seems almost undercooked, 30 to 35 minutes. (It will jiggle a little, and when you spoon into the cake, it may separate into 2 layers: a cakey, custardy layer and an oatmealy layer. This is actual magic.)

Spoon into bowls and serve warm.

with hot water:

SERVES 8

PREP TIME: 15 minutes **TOTAL TIME:** 7 hours 30 minutes

FRENCH TOAST CASSEROLE
WITH SALTED FROSTED FLAKES

for the **BASE**

- 1 tablespoon softened butter, for greasing the baking dish
- 1-pound loaf French bread, cut into 1½-inch cubes (stale or day-old is fine!)
- 8 large eggs
- 2 cups heavy cream
- 1 cup whole milk
- ½ cup spiced rum (because rum for breakfast)
- 1 cup (packed) light brown sugar
- 1 tablespoon vanilla extract
- 1 teaspoon ground cinnamon
- ½ teaspoon grated nutmeg
- ½ teaspoon kosher salt

for the **TOPPING**

- 3 cups Frosted Flakes cereal
- 3 tablespoons butter, melted
- ½ teaspoon kosher salt

I am so proud of this dish I could cry. It took a lot of time to perfect it, but oh, was it worth it. I mean it has a freaking Frosted-Flakes-tossed-in-butter-and-salt topping. It is inner-fat-kid madness. The bread needs a lot of time to soak, so throw it all together before your night of debauchery and use its magical powers (rum) to cure yourself in the morning. (Afternoon. Who are we kidding?)

MAKE THE BASE: Butter a 9 × 13-inch baking dish (or a tall-sided 12-inch ovenproof skillet) and arrange the cubed bread in the dish.

In a big bowl, whisk the eggs to combine, then whisk in the heavy cream, milk, rum, brown sugar, vanilla, cinnamon, nutmeg, and salt until smooth. Pour the mixture over the bread, pressing on the bread to help soak it in the custard. Refrigerate for at least 6 hours and up to 12.

Preheat the oven to 350°F. Take the casserole out of the fridge and let it sit at room temp for 30 minutes.

MAKE THE TOPPING: In a bowl, combine the cereal, melted butter, and salt and toss to coat. Spread the mixture evenly over the casserole.

Bake until the topping is golden and the bread cubes peeking out of the top are crusty and toasty, 50 to 55 minutes.

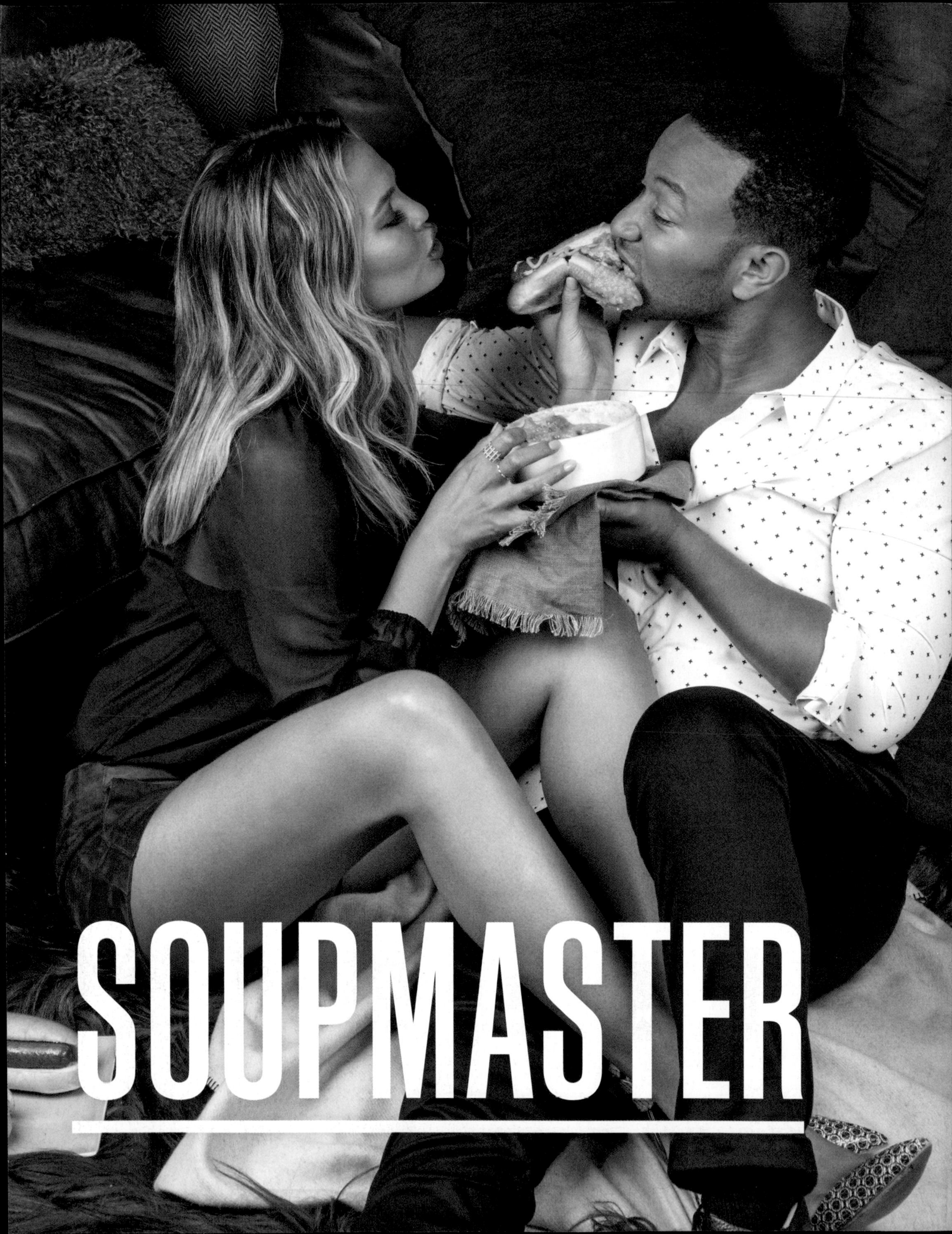

SOUPMASTER

// *Opposite:* Split Pea Soup with Crispy Hot Dogs (PAGE 53)

SERVES 4

PREP TIME: 25 minutes **TOTAL TIME:** 1 hour 45 minutes

ROASTED TOMATO SOUP

for the **TOMATOES**

- 4 pounds ripe tomatoes (Roma, plum, vine-ripened, whatever)
- ¼ cup extra-virgin olive oil
- 1 tablespoon kosher salt
- ½ teaspoon freshly ground black pepper

for the **SOUP**

- 3 herb sprigs (rosemary, thyme, oregano, whatever), plus more for garnish
- 2 tablespoons extra-virgin olive oil
- 1 small onion, finely diced
- 5 cloves garlic, minced
- 2½ cups low-sodium chicken broth
- Kosher salt and freshly ground black pepper

Oh, how I love thee. I get excited just thinking about pulling a tray of perfectly roasted tomatoes, sizzling in olive oil, out of the oven. The smell fills your house, and you're still on step one. Tomato soup, in all its simple glory, tastes like love. I can't imagine a human being who wouldn't love every spoonful of this soup.

ROAST THE TOMATOES: Preheat the oven to 450°F. Line a baking sheet with foil.

Core and halve the tomatoes (or quarter if they're big). Arrange the tomatoes, cut-side up, on the baking sheet. Drizzle with the oil, then sprinkle with the salt and pepper. Roast until softened and the edges are charred, 35 to 40 minutes.

MAKE THE SOUP: Tie the herbs with a piece of twine into an herb bundle.

In a large saucepan, heat the oil over medium-high heat. Add the onion and cook, stirring, until softened, 6 to 8 minutes. Add the garlic and cook 1 more minute. Add the roasted tomatoes to the pan and break them up with a spoon. Add the broth and herb bundle and bring to a boil, then reduce the heat and simmer until thickened, 25 to 30 minutes.

Discard the herbs. Transfer the soup to a blender and puree until almost smooth but a few chunks remain. Season to taste with salt and pepper. Use your powers as a SoupMaster responsibly.

SERVES 8

PREP TIME: 20 minutes **TOTAL TIME:** 1 hour 20 minutes

ROTOCHICK CHICKEN NOODLE SOUP

- **2 tablespoons extra-virgin olive oil**
- **1 medium onion, chopped**
- **5 medium carrots, cut into coins (2 cups)**
- **6 celery stalks, cut into half moons (2 cups)**
- **2 tablespoons minced garlic (about 4 cloves)**
- **1 teaspoon chopped fresh thyme**
- **Kosher salt and freshly ground black pepper**
- **1 bay leaf**
- **10 cups low-sodium chicken broth**
- **2 cups cooked wide egg noodles (about 3 ounces dried noodles)**
- **2½ cups mixed shredded dark and light rotochick meat (from a large rotisserie chicken)**

My friend Melissa once called store-bought rotisserie chickens "rotochicks," and I haven't called them anything else since. When I'm in a mood and a half, I usually want chicken soup, but in those moments, roasting a chicken isn't exactly a high priority. So using the rotochick isn't a cheat move—it's a conscious decision that will make everyone happier.

Growing up, I'd make this soup with my dad, and he would reheat it all week long. Sitting at the table, I'd thickly butter what felt like hundreds of saltine crackers and slide them over to him one by one. To this day, this soup doesn't feel right to me without them, and the last sip of soup is like a buttery, brothy dessert. Oh baby.

In a big soup pot, heat the oil over medium-high heat. Add the onion and cook, stirring, until softened, 6 to 8 minutes. Add the carrots, celery, garlic, thyme, 1 tablespoon salt, and 1 teaspoon pepper and cook, stirring, until the carrots soften slightly, about 5 minutes. Add the bay leaf and chicken broth and bring to a boil. Reduce the heat and simmer for 45 minutes to meld the flavors.

Stir in the noodles and chicken and simmer for 5 to 10 minutes longer. Season to taste with more salt and pepper and discard the bay leaf. Serve with buttered saltines, if you want to be like me and my dad.

SERVES 4 TO 6

PREP TIME: 20 minutes **TOTAL TIME:** 50 minutes

CHUNKY CREAMY MUSHROOM SOUP

- **4 tablespoons (½ stick) unsalted butter, plus 4 to 6 pats for serving**
- **1 small onion, finely chopped**
- **6 cloves garlic, minced**
- **3 pounds assorted mushrooms, trimmed and finely chopped (see Note)**
- **1 tablespoon chopped fresh thyme or ½ tablespoon dried, plus more for garnish**
- **Kosher salt and freshly ground black pepper**
- **2 cups low-sodium chicken broth, plus more if necessary**

note You can finely chop the mushrooms by hand or by pulsing in the food processor in batches.

Ever heard the term skinny-fat? It means being relatively thin but pretty much having 90 percent body fat, a.k.a. me. That is why I call this soup chunky creamy. It speaks to me.

Mushrooms are savory dirt growths that I cannot get enough of, and I'm convinced that mushroom haters are that way because they've only had them raw. But this soup cooks them down and screams comfort and flavor. Get crazy and experiment with different medleys of mushrooms. Oh man, I really am married now. This is not how I used to get crazy with mushrooms.

Get out a big soup pot (the soup will shrink down, but it starts out big because mushrooms lose a lot of their water when cooking). Heat the butter in the pot over medium-high heat. Add the onion and cook, stirring, until softened, about 8 minutes. Add the garlic and cook 1 more minute. Add the mushrooms, thyme, 2 teaspoons salt, and ¼ teaspoon pepper and cook, stirring, until the mushrooms release their water and shrink to half their size, about 10 minutes. Add the broth and bring to a boil, then reduce the heat and simmer until the mushrooms are super tender and the soup thickens slightly, 15 to 20 minutes.

Puree half of the soup (about 3 cups) in a blender or food processor until smooth, then stir it back into the pot. Thin with additional broth if needed, and season to taste with salt and pepper.

Serve in mugs or bowls and top each one with a pat of butter and some thyme.

SERVES 6

PREP TIME: 25 minutes **TOTAL TIME:** 1 hour 30 minutes

BUTTERNUT SQUASH SOUP WITH PROSCIUTTO CRISPS

While most butternut squash soups are a little too sweet for my liking, this one is all caramelized goodness. Crisping the sage and prosciutto takes every spoonful to the next level—I love to hide half of it on the bottom of each bowl for maximum ribbed pleasure for him and her in every bite.

- **2 small or 1 large butternut squash (about 3½ pounds), peeled, seeded, and cut into 1-inch cubes**
- **5 tablespoons extra-virgin olive oil, plus more for frying the sage**
- **1 tablespoon kosher salt**
- **1 teaspoon freshly ground black pepper**
- **4 cups low-sodium chicken broth**
- **16 sage leaves**
- **1 medium onion, chopped**
- **1 tablespoon minced garlic (about 2 cloves)**
- **¾ cup heavy cream, plus a little more for serving**
- **6 Prosciutto Crisps (recipe follows)**

In a large bowl, toss together the squash, 1 tablespoon of the oil, the salt, and pepper.

In the biggest soup pot you have, heat 2 tablespoons of the oil over medium-high heat. Add half the squash, spread it out in one layer (or close to it) and let it sit there (don't move it) until the underside gets nice and dark brown, 6 to 7 minutes. Using a metal spatula, lift the squash, scraping the bottom of the pot as much as possible, and try to flip the squash, but don't worry if you don't flip it all. Continue to cook the squash until the underside is browned, 5 to 6 minutes. Add just enough of the broth to dissolve the sticky bits in the pot and dump it all into a big bowl. Rinse and wipe the pot out and repeat the cooking with the remaining squash and 2 tablespoons oil, only leave this batch in the pot when it's done.

Finely chop 4 of the sage leaves and add to the pot. Add the onion and garlic and cook, scraping the bottom of the pan to loosen those yummy browned bits, until the onions are soft and lightly golden, 9 minutes. Add the previous batch of squash and the remaining broth and bring to a boil. Reduce the heat and simmer until the squash is tender and starting to fall apart, about 25 minutes.

While the soup is simmering, in a small saucepan, heat about ½ inch of olive oil over medium heat until shimmering-hot. Working in batches of a few leaves at a time, add the sage to the hot oil and watch them crisp up; it will only take 10 to 15 seconds. You'll know they're ready when they stop sizzling but are still a pretty, green, sage-y color. As each batch is done, remove and drain on paper towels.

Transfer the soup to a blender and blend until almost smooth; a few chunks are OK (do this in batches if necessary, and use a towel to protect your hand from hot splashes). Return the soup to the pot, add the cream, and simmer until warmed through, about 5 minutes.

Divide the soup among 6 bowls, swirl a spoonful of cream into each one, and top each bowl with a prosciutto crisp and 2 crispy sage leaves.

prosciutto crisps

As many pieces of thin-sliced prosciutto as you want

Preheat the oven to 400°F. Line a baking sheet with parchment paper.

Arrange the prosciutto in a single layer on the baking sheet. Bake until wrinkled and slightly shrunken, 11 to 13 minutes. (It will crisp as it cools.) Cool, eat whole as a snack, or crumble and use as a garnish for salads, eggs, or anything that could use crispness and ham. (Everything.)

SERVES 10 TO 12

PREP TIME: 30 minutes **TOTAL TIME:** 1 hour 45 minutes

POT PIE SOUP
WITH CRUST CRACKERS

for the **PIE CRUST**

- 2 sticks (8 ounces) cold unsalted butter, cubed
- 2½ cups all-purpose flour, plus more for dusting
- 1 teaspoon fine sea salt
- ½ cup ice water

for the **SOUP**

- 6 cups low-sodium chicken broth
- 2 cups whole milk
- 2 sticks (8 ounces) unsalted butter, cut into chunks
- 2 tablespoons minced garlic (about 3 cloves)
- 1 cup all-purpose flour
- 4 teaspoons kosher salt, plus more to taste
- 1½ teaspoons freshly ground black pepper, or more to taste
- 1 large russet (Idaho) potato, peeled and cut into ½-inch cubes
- ½ pound diced carrots (2 cups)
- 1 cup frozen peas
- 1 cup frozen pearl onions
- ¼ pound deli ham, thinly sliced
- 1 pound skinless rotisserie chicken meat, cubed (3 cups)
- ½ cup heavy cream

Chicken pot pie is one of my favorite things on God's green earth. Same goes for Dad, whose Twitter is 99 percent reviews of frozen pot pies and includes a header background of his personal favorite, the $0.99 Swanson version. I love soup, so I wanted to make one inspired by chicken pot pie, without, you know, having to make a pot pie. But I neeeeeed, I crave, that crust. The crust that I crack and mix into the creamy filling—the golden brown edges I save for scooping up the corners of the ramekin. So why not have it all? We decided to make a single slab of crust and break it up so that Every. Single. Bite. Can be scooped up with the crust I so desire.

This needs to be in some sort of hall of fame. It needs a ribbon in the county fair, its own show on TLC.

They will literally put anything on television.

MAKE THE PIE CRUST: You might think the butter is cold, but after you cube it, put it back in the fridge for at least 20 minutes.

In a food processor, pulse the flour and sea salt until incorporated. Add the cold butter and pulse until just pea-size pieces of butter remain, 15 to 20 pulses. Add the ice water and pulse until a dough just forms, 15 to 20 pulses.

Dust your work surface with some flour. Turn the dough out of the processor bowl and gather the dough into two 5-inch discs and wrap in plastic wrap. Freeze one of the discs for another use (it will last for weeks in the freezer if you wrapped it nice and tight). Chill the other dough disc in the refrigerator for at least 30 minutes (you can keep the dough in the fridge for up to 2 days).

Preheat the oven to 375°F.

// *recipe continues*

Place the dough on a piece of parchment paper. Using a floured rolling pin, roll the disc into a 12-inch round (it doesn't have to be perfect). Prick it all over with a fork. Put the dough, with the parchment, on a baking sheet and bake until golden and crisp, about 30 minutes.

Cool thoroughly and break into pieces.

MAKE THE SOUP: In a saucepan, bring the broth and milk to a simmer and keep at a simmer.

In a big soup pot, heat the butter over medium-high heat until foamy. Add the garlic and cook, stirring, until fragrant, about 1 minute. Add the flour, reduce the heat to medium, and cook, stirring, until toasty and foaming, 2 to 3 minutes. Whisk in the broth-milk mixture, slowly at first, then add the salt and pepper. Bring to a boil, then reduce the heat and cook until thickened, about 5 minutes. Add the potato, carrots, peas, pearl onions, and ham and simmer until the potatoes are tender, about 20 minutes. Stir in the chicken and cream and heat through for 5 additional minutes. Season with salt and pepper to taste and serve with the broken pie crust on the side.

SERVES 8 TO 10

PREP TIME: 15 minutes **TOTAL TIME:** 1 hour 30 minutes

SPLIT PEA SOUP WITH CRISPY HOT DOGS

You are hesitant. I can feel it from here. You don't want to love this but I promise you, you'll be left with no choice. I grew up eating split pea soup straight out of the can. When I would cook it, I would sit up on the counter, roll up deli ham, and dip it into the pot because pea fondue is what classy people do. (Noting for future rap lyric.) But I'm grown now. And grown people use hot dogs. OK, so I'm not selling it well. Just make it. It's literally ridiculously good. (See photograph, page 40.)

- 3 tablespoons extra-virgin olive oil
- 1 large onion, chopped
- 6 hot dogs, thinly sliced
- 4 medium carrots, cut into coins
- 4 celery stalks, cut into half-moons
- 2 tablespoons minced garlic (about 4 cloves)
- Kosher salt and freshly ground black pepper
- 1 pound dried green split peas, rinsed
- 1 bay leaf
- Hot Dog Bun Croutons (recipe follows), for garnish

In a big soup pot, heat the oil over medium-high heat. Add the onion and most of the hot dogs (reserve about ½ cup of the hot dogs for garnish) and cook, stirring, until the onion is translucent, 7 to 9 minutes. Add the carrots, celery, garlic, 1 tablespoon salt, and 1 teaspoon pepper and cook, stirring, until the carrots soften slightly, about 8 minutes.

Add the split peas, bay leaf, and 9 cups water and bring to a boil. Reduce the heat and simmer until the split peas break up and become creamy, 50 to 55 minutes. (Cook it a little longer and it gets a little creamier.) Season to taste with salt and pepper and discard the bay leaf.

Meanwhile, throw the reserved hot dogs in a small dry skillet over medium-high heat and let them crisp up and get charred, shaking the skillet once in a while, 5 to 6 minutes.

Serve the soup garnished with the crispy hot dogs and the croutons.

hot dog bun croutons

- 2 tablespoons butter
- 2 hot dog buns, cut into ½-inch dice
- Kosher salt and freshly ground black pepper

In a medium skillet, melt the butter over medium heat. Add the diced buns and cook, stirring, until golden and the edges are crisped, 5 to 6 minutes. Transfer to a plate and season to taste with salt and pepper.

SERVES 6 TO 8

PREP TIME: 15 minutes **TOTAL TIME:** 1 hour 15 minutes

(JOHN WAS SKEPTICAL ABOUT THIS) VEGETABLE TORTILLA STEW

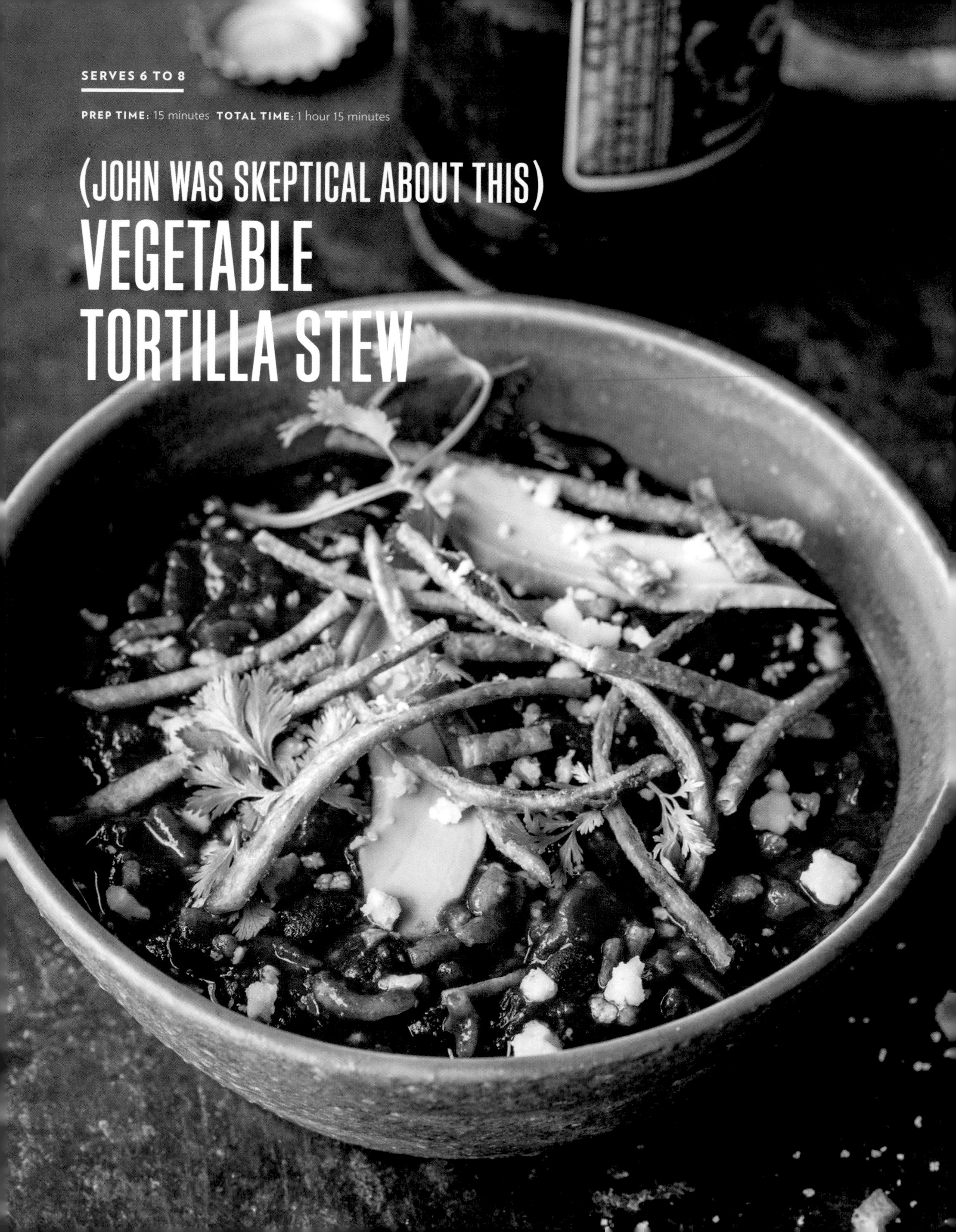

for the **STEW**

- 2 tablespoons vegetable oil
- 1 large onion, diced
- 1 large green bell pepper, diced
- 1 large jalapeño pepper, finely diced (include the seeds)
- 2 tablespoons minced garlic (about 4 cloves)
- 2 tablespoons chili powder
- 1 tablespoon ground cumin
- ½ teaspoon cayenne pepper
- Kosher salt and freshly ground black pepper
- 4 cups low-sodium vegetable or chicken broth
- 2 (15-ounce) cans diced tomatoes in juice
- 2 (15-ounce) cans black beans, drained and rinsed
- 1 cup cooked rice

for the **TORTILLA STRIPPIES**

- 2 cups vegetable oil, for frying
- 4 corn tortillas
- Kosher salt

for **SERVING**

- Roughly chopped fresh cilantro leaves
- 1 avocado, sliced
- Crumbled cotija or shredded cheddar cheese

Ohhhhh my god it was hard to not throw chicken into this, but I was dead set on giving my vegetarian loves something even my meat-loving butt could be blown away by. I love every damned thing in this book, but there are some I can actually taste when I write about them or merely look at a photo. This is one of those recipes. Full of veggie goodness and the perfect amount of kick. Thick enough for chip dipping but perfect for a spoonful all up in your mouth. I don't even know how you're still reading this unless you can safely read a hardcover while driving to the grocery store.

MAKE THE STEW: In a soup pot, heat the oil over medium heat until shimmering. Add the onion, bell pepper, and jalapeño and cook, stirring, until the onion is translucent and a teeny bit golden, about 10 minutes. Add the garlic, chili powder, cumin, cayenne, 2 teaspoons salt, and ½ teaspoon black pepper and cook, stirring until fragrant, about 2 minutes. Add the chicken broth, tomatoes, and beans and bring to a boil. Reduce the heat and simmer for 30 minutes. Add the rice and cook until the stew gets nice and thick, about 15 minutes more. Season with more salt, pepper, and spice, if you want.

MAKE THE TORTILLA STRIPPIES: Fill a small or medium saucepan with a couple inches of oil and heat over medium-high heat. Stack the tortillas on top of each other and cut them into thin strips using a sharp knife. Test the oil by dropping a tortilla strip in; if it sizzles immediately, you're good to go. A small handful at a time, gently lower the strips into the oil and fry until crisp, 1 to 2 minutes. Pull them out with a slotted spoon, drain on paper towels, and salt 'em up.

To serve, divide the soup among bowls and garnish with cilantro, avocado, cheese, and the tortilla strippies.

SALADS (FOR WHEN YOU NEED THEM)

Opposite: Shaved Brussels Sprouts with Grapes and Almonds (PAGE 68)

SERVES 6

PREP TIME: 10 minutes **TOTAL TIME:** 20 minutes

CAPRESE SALAD
WITH CRISPY PROSCIUTTO

4 cups baby arugula
1 (8-ounce) ball burrata cheese
2 pounds ripe tomatoes, cut in a variety of shapes (wedges, slices, chunks, etc.)
3 tablespoons really good olive oil
1 tablespoon balsamic vinegar
2 teaspoons kosher salt
½ teaspoon freshly ground black pepper
6 Prosciutto Crisps (page 49)

It's no secret that my heart lies in Italy. John loves the way they sing their sentences. We morrrrre than love their food. I love an Italian man. John loves an Italian woman. We fell in love in Italy, we were married in Italy. The list is endless. Italy finds such beauty in simplicity. And there is nothing more simple than plopping a ball of burrata cheese (it's like mozzarella, but on creamy drugs) onto a gorgeous plate of heirloom tomatoes. Crisping the prosciutto adds another dimension that I can't live without. Tomatoes and cheese, yes please.

Scatter the arugula on a serving platter and place the burrata ball in the center. Arrange the tomatoes around the burrata. Break open the burrata ball a little so you can see the creamy center, then drizzle all around the platter with the olive oil. Drizzle the tomatoes and arugula with balsamic vinegar. Season the entire salad with the salt and pepper and top with the prosciutto crisps.

SERVES 6

PREP TIME: 20 minutes **TOTAL TIME:** 40 minutes

IL BUCO-STYLE KALE SALAD

for the **CROUTONS**

- ¼ cup olive oil
- 1 tablespoon very finely minced garlic (about 2 cloves)
- 1 teaspoon kosher salt
- ½ teaspoon freshly ground black pepper
- ¼ cup finely grated Parmigiano-Reggiano cheese
- 4 cups cubed (1-inch) day-old French loaf or country loaf

for the **DRESSING**

- ⅓ cup extra-virgin olive oil
- ¼ cup fresh lemon juice
- 1 teaspoon kosher salt
- ½ teaspoon freshly ground black pepper

for the **SALAD**

- Kosher salt
- 1½ pounds dinosaur (lacinato) kale
- ½ cup finely grated Parmigiano-Reggiano cheese
- ¼ teaspoon freshly ground black pepper

I so badly want to hate kale, but that endeavor is impossible once you try these Caesar(ish) leafy bastards. There's a little restaurant on Bond Street in NYC—a dream street I would love to one day live on—called Il Buco. It is home to our first date, our first fights, our first food favorites. Many a booze-fueled lunch. One time I threw up so hard into their toilet that I hit my forehead and had to wear fake bangs for a week. Memories! Anyhoo, their kale Caesar taught me that it is, indeed, possible to love kale. Sure, it's covered in giant garlic croutons and heaps of Parmesan, but bitch, don't kill my vibe.

MAKE THE CROUTONS: Preheat the oven to 350°F.

In a large bowl, whisk together the oil, garlic, salt, pepper, and Parm. Add the bread and toss to coat. Transfer to a baking sheet and bake until golden, 20 to 22 minutes. Remove from the oven and cool.

MAKE THE DRESSING: In a small bowl, whisk together the oil, lemon juice, salt, and pepper. Set aside.

PREPARE THE SALAD: Bring a large pot of well-salted water to a boil. Fill a large bowl with ice and water. Throw the kale into the boiling water in batches, until it turns bright green, about 5 seconds, then remove with tongs or a slotted spoon and place in the ice water bath. Dry the kale really well in a salad spinner or between layers of paper towels (this is really important). Tear the kale leaves off the tough stalks, cut the leaves into 2-inch pieces, and transfer to a salad bowl. (Save the stalks for another use, or discard.)

Add the dressing to the kale and toss well. Add half the Parm and toss well, so the cheese makes the dressing seem almost creamy. Toss with half the croutons. Top the salad with the rest of the cheese and croutons. Season with the pepper and some salt, if desired.

ROASTED CAULIFLOWER, FETA, AND ORZO SALAD

SERVES 4 TO 6

PREP TIME: 20 minutes **TOTAL TIME:** 45 minutes

I have my closest girlfriends over whenever possible. The only way I can even kiiiiind of make up for the countless missed milestones and baby births and weddings is by showering them with gift-bag-giveaway parties or having our wonderfully talented and hilarious friend Chef Roblé (and Adam! Hi, Adam!) come over and teach us a few things.

This salad is one of the best things he has ever made for us. It sits out well on the counter for parties, it's beautiful, and it's full of flavor you can feel free to have fun with—add different nuts and dried berries, some quinoa, or chia seeds (if you wanna ruin it in the name of fiber).

for the **CAULIFLOWER AND ORZO**

- 1 small head cauliflower, broken into small florets (about 5 cups)
- 4 tablespoons olive oil
- 3 cloves garlic, minced
- 1 teaspoon kosher salt
- ½ teaspoon freshly ground black pepper
- 1 cup orzo pasta

for the **DRESSING AND SALAD**

- 3 tablespoons extra-virgin olive oil
- 3 tablespoons fresh lemon juice
- 1 teaspoon honey
- 1 teaspoon Dijon mustard
- ½ teaspoon kosher salt, plus more to taste
- ½ teaspoon freshly ground black pepper
- ¼ cup thinly sliced red onion
- 1 cup crumbled feta cheese (see Note)
- ⅔ cup dried cherries
- 4 cups baby spinach

PREPARE THE CAULIFLOWER AND ORZO: Preheat the oven to 400°F.

In a bowl, toss the cauliflower with 3 tablespoons of the olive oil, the garlic, salt, and pepper. Spread on a rimmed baking sheet and roast until softened and the edges are charred, 20 to 25 minutes. Let cool and set aside.

Meanwhile, in a pot of salted boiling water, cook the orzo according to the package directions, but for 1 or 2 minutes less than called for (so it's just a little underdone). Drain in a colander, rinse under cold water, drain well, and toss with the remaining 1 tablespoon oil right in the colander.

MAKE THE DRESSING AND TOSS THE SALAD: In a big bowl, whisk together the olive oil, lemon juice, honey, mustard, salt, and pepper. Add the cooked orzo, roasted cauliflower, onion, feta, and cherries and toss until coated with the dressing. Throw the spinach on top and toss one more time. Taste, and add more salt if you'd like.

note // The French kind of feta cheese is a little creamier and milder, the Greek is a little saltier. Take your pick.

SERVES 4 TO 6

TOTAL TIME: 20 minutes

SRIRACHA CAESAR SALAD

I travel so much that there is absolutely no consistency in my life whatsoever. Once, when I was in the midst of a mental breakdown, a dear friend had one word of advice for me: Floss. Literally one word. She was basically saying that if I made the effort to floss every single night before bed, no matter how wild my day, it would bring some sense of normalcy to an otherwise abnormal life.

Caesar salad is my food dental floss, the only other constant in my life. No matter where I go, where I stay, Caesar's on the menu. I have had it in every country, and I feel confident in saying that the twist of spice makes this the best Caesar salad I have ever, ever had. So go ahead. Floss.

for the **TOASTS**

- 2 tablespoons olive oil
- 4 cloves garlic, very finely minced or mashed into a paste
- ¼ teaspoon red pepper flakes
- ½ teaspoon salt
- ¼ teaspoon freshly ground black pepper
- 12 thin slices baguette

for the **SALAD**

- 8 cups chopped baby romaine lettuce spears
- 1 cup halved cherry tomatoes, or quartered if large
- ¼ cup thinly sliced red onion
- Sriracha Caesar Dressing (recipe follows)
- ¼ cup shaved Parmigiano-Reggiano
- Kosher salt and freshly ground black pepper

MAKE THE TOASTS: Preheat the oven to 350°F. Line a baking sheet with foil.

In a small bowl, combine the oil, garlic, red pepper flakes, salt, and pepper. Arrange the baguette slices on the baking sheet and brush with the oil mixture. Bake until browned and crisp, 11 to 12 minutes. Cool.

ASSEMBLE THE SALAD: Arrange the lettuce, tomatoes, and onion on a big platter. Drizzle with dressing to taste, then crumble the garlic toasts on top of the platter and scatter with the Parm shavings. Season with salt and pepper and more cheese.

sriracha caesar dressing

MAKES ABOUT 2CUPS

1 cup mayonnaise
4 cloves garlic, smashed
1½ cups finely grated Parmigiano-Reggiano cheese
2 tablespoons fresh lemon juice
1 tablespoon Sriracha, or more to taste
1½ teaspoons anchovy paste
1½ teaspoons Dijon mustard
1 teaspoon Worcestershire sauce
¼ teaspoon kosher salt
¼ teaspoon freshly ground black pepper

In a food processor or blender, combine the mayo, garlic, Parm, lemon juice, Sriracha, anchovy paste, mustard, Worcestershire sauce, salt, and pepper and process until smooth. Refrigerate until ready to use. The dressing will keep in the fridge for 2 weeks or so. Put it on anything. Eat lots of Caesar. Floss.

SERVES 2 AS A MAIN COURSE or 4 AS A SIDE DISH OR APPETIZER

TOTAL TIME: 30 minutes

CHINESE CHICKEN SALAD
WITH CRISPY WONTON SKINS

for the
CRISPY WONTONS

- 3 (8-inch) square wonton wrappers or 6 (4-inch) square wrappers
- Vegetable oil, for frying
- Kosher salt

for the
DRESSING

- ⅓ cup peanut or vegetable oil
- ⅓ cup unseasoned rice vinegar
- 1 tablespoon Chinese hot mustard
- 1 tablespoon light soy sauce
- 1 teaspoon Sriracha
- 1 teaspoon sesame oil
- 1 tablespoon honey
- 3 cloves garlic
- ½ teaspoon kosher salt

for the
SALAD

- ½ rotisserie chicken
- ½ medium head napa cabbage, cut into ½-inch slices (6 cups)
- 1 cup shredded red cabbage
- 1 cup cilantro leaves, roughly chopped
- 1 small carrot, cut into julienne strips
- ½ cup thinly sliced red onion
- 4 scallions, thinly sliced

Don't say this to the TSA, but airport food is the f*cking b*mb. I know this goes against everything you've heard, but I gotta say, some of my most memorable meals have been at airports. Maybe it's because I go in with zero expectations, but I'd like to think it's more about the random drunken company and the extreme diversity in . . . dare I say it . . . cuisine. LAX has a Kogi Truck. Literally a Korean BBQ taco truck, with wheels, inside the Delta terminal. SFO is home to delicious meatballs at Cat Cora's. Austin has me finding myself sucking on Salt Lick ribs while listening to someone simultaneously playing the harmonica and banjo as I sit in a rocking chair.

And in a rush, many airports are home to my go-to, bring-on-the-plane Wolfgang Puck Chinois Chicken Salad. Shredded veggies on crunchy romaine, wontons IN A BAG SO THEY DON'T GET SOGGY—WHY CAN'T ANYONE BUT WOLFGANG FIGURE THIS OUT I DO NOT KNOW—and a dressing so delightful you may buy two salads just to double up on it.

So either buy a plane ticket to somewhere and enjoy your $600 salad, or make the damn thing at home over and over again, because I promise, you will want this all. The. Time.

MAKE THE CRISPY WONTONS: Stack the wonton wrappers on top of each other. Cut the wrappers into strips ½ inch wide and 4 inches long. (If you're using the 8-inch wrappers, first cut them in half into 4 × 8-inch rectangles.)

In a medium saucepan, heat 3 inches of oil over medium-high heat until one of the strips puffs up and sizzles as soon as it hits the oil. Working in batches, drop a handful of the wonton strips at a time into the oil and fry until puffed and golden, about 30 seconds. Using a slotted spoon, transfer the fried strips to paper towels and sprinkle generously with salt. Repeat until done.

MAKE THE DRESSING: In a blender, combine the peanut oil, rice vinegar, mustard, soy sauce, Sriracha, sesame oil, honey, garlic, and salt and blend until smooth. Trust me, you want to bust out the blender for this to make it all smooth and creamy.

MAKE THE SALAD: Remove the skin from the chicken and discard. Using your hands, shred the meat into very thin pieces you would want to eat in a salad (about 3 cups of meat in the end).

Place the meat in a bowl with the napa and red cabbages, cilantro, carrot, red onion, and scallions. Pour in ½ cup of the dressing, toss to coat, and top with the wonton skins. Serve the remaining dressing on the side for salad touch-ups.

SERVES 6

TOTAL TIME: 25 minutes

SHAVED BRUSSELS SPROUTS
WITH GRAPES AND ALMONDS

- **1 pound Brussels spouts**
- **¼ cup fresh lemon juice**
- **3 tablespoons extra-virgin olive oil**
- **½ cup finely grated Parmigiano-Reggiano cheese**
- **¾ teaspoon freshly ground black pepper**
- **½ teaspoon kosher salt**
- **1½ cups grapes, halved**
- **½ cup slivered almonds, toasted**

Despite never knowing they're "BrusselSSSSS" sprouts, I have been a lover of them since I grew teeth. And John is one Brussels sprouts–loving SOB. So in order to keep our Brussels sprouts sex life spicy, I am constantly trying to find new ways to doll them up. But sometimes things are just easy. He loves salad. He loves sprouts. He loves grapes. He loves nuts. So he loves this salad. Men. Don't overthink it.

Using a mandoline or a sharp knife, cut the Brussels sprouts into really thin shreds. Rinse them with ice cold water (this crisps and cleans the sprouts) and dry well in a salad spinner, or roll them in layers of paper towels.

In a large bowl, whisk together the lemon juice, olive oil, Parm, pepper, and salt. Add the Brussels sprouts, grapes, and almonds and gently toss.

SERVES 4

TOTAL TIME: 20 minutes

BUTTER LETTUCE
WITH BLUE CHEESE AND CAYENNE-CANDIED WALNUTS

Easily one of my favorite things in this book. I can't imagine a single dish this wouldn't go with. Plus, the cayenne-candied nuts take every bite to the next level. I suggest making a double batch—for the salad and to pop into your mouth all week long. Also, a secret from me to you: The best candied nuts I have ever had come from a little (well rather large, actually) stand inside the Farmers Market at The Grove in L.A. They're called Magic Nuts. So salty and so sweet, one bag makes me magically have to lie down to put my pants on for a week.

for the **DRESSING**

- 3 tablespoons extra-virgin olive oil
- 2 tablespoons red wine vinegar
- ¼ cup blue cheese crumbles
- 1 small shallot, finely chopped
- ¼ teaspoon kosher salt
- ¼ teaspoon freshly ground black pepper

for the **SALAD**

- 1 large head butter or Boston lettuce, separated into leaves, larger leaves torn
- 1 apple, halved and cut into thin slices
- ½ small red onion, sliced into thin rings
- ½ cup Cayenne-Candied Walnuts (recipe follows)

MAKE THE DRESSING: In a bowl, whisk together the olive oil, vinegar, blue cheese, shallot, salt, and pepper.

ASSEMBLE THE SALAD: In a salad bowl, combine the lettuce, apple, and onion. Drizzle in the dressing to taste, toss lightly, and top with the cayenne-candied walnuts. Any extra dressing keeps for a week in the fridge.

cayenne-candied walnuts

MAKES ABOUT 1 CUP

- 1 cup walnut halves
- ¼ cup sugar
- 1 tablespoon butter
- ¼ teaspoon kosher salt, plus more to taste
- ⅛ teaspoon freshly ground black pepper, plus more to taste
- ¼ teaspoon cayenne pepper, plus more to taste

In a nonstick skillet, combine the walnuts, sugar, butter, salt, and black pepper. Cook over medium heat, stirring, until the sugar melts, coats the nuts, and darkens, 5 to 6 minutes. Transfer to a plate and sprinkle with the cayenne. Let cool, then break apart. Season with more salt, black pepper, or cayenne, if desired.

SERVES 6

PREP TIME: 20 minutes **TOTAL TIME:** 40 minutes

COBB SALAD
WITH HONEY-MUSTARD RANCH DRESSING

I know this salad is good because it gets me more Instagram likes than my boobs. While most people on earth have not tried my boobs and this salad side by side, I think the figures are right here. The chicken is our no-fail baked chicken breast, perfectly seasoned. (I absolutely loathe salads that throw in dry, boiled chicken breast. Do it right!) And why honey-mustard ranch? Because I love both honey mustard and ranch and couldn't decide. So we made them haves the sex and oh man, did they make a beautiful baby.

for the **CHICKEN AND CORN**

- Olive oil
- 1½ teaspoons paprika
- 1 teaspoon kosher salt
- ¾ teaspoon ground cumin
- ¼ teaspoon thyme leaves
- ¼ teaspoon freshly ground black pepper
- ¼ teaspoon cayenne pepper
- 2 boneless, skinless chicken breasts (about ¾ pound)
- 1 (15-ounce) can corn kernels, drained and patted dry

for the **DRESSING**

- ½ cup mayonnaise
- ¼ cup buttermilk
- 2 tablespoons Dijon mustard
- 2 teaspoons honey
- ½ teaspoon dried oregano
- ½ teaspoon garlic powder
- ¼ teaspoon onion powder
- ¼ teaspoon paprika
- Pinch of cayenne pepper
- ¾ teaspoon kosher salt
- ½ teaspoon freshly ground black pepper

for the **SALAD**

- 1 head iceberg lettuce, chopped
- 1 cup cherry tomatoes, halved
- 1 large avocado, cubed
- 10 slices bacon, cooked (see Note) and crumbled
- 4 hard-boiled eggs (see Note), chopped

COOK THE CHICKEN AND CORN: Preheat the oven to 350°F. Line a baking sheet with foil and lightly coat with oil.

In a small bowl, combine 1 tablespoon oil, paprika, salt, cumin, thyme, black pepper, and cayenne. Rub the mixture all over the chicken. Place the chicken on the baking sheet and bake until cooked through but still juicy, 15 to 20 minutes. Transfer the chicken to a plate and when cool enough to handle, cut into small bite-size pieces.

Meanwhile, arrange the corn on the same baking sheet. Crank up the heat to broil and broil the corn until just slightly charred, 5 to 6 minutes. Remove from the oven and cool.

MAKE THE DRESSING: In a small bowl, stir together the mayo, buttermilk, mustard, honey, oregano, garlic powder, onion powder, paprika, cayenne, salt, and black pepper. Refrigerate until ready to use.

ASSEMBLE THE SALAD: Arrange the lettuce on a serving platter or in a big salad bowl. Top with the tomatoes, avocado, bacon, roasted corn, eggs, and chicken. If you're like me, line them up in the most OCD way possible and get really annoyed when the lines aren't perfectly straight. Drizzle the dressing to taste over the salad, and toss if you want to ruin all those pretty lines. Serve immediately. Any leftover dressing keeps in the fridge for a week or so.

note

The best way to cook bacon is on a baking sheet, the way I do it for Garlic-Roasted Bacon (page 17) . . . minus the garlic. And the best way to hard boil eggs is in the Secretly Spicy Deviled Eggs (page 132).

SERVES 8

PREP TIME: 5 minutes **TOTAL TIME:** 3 hours

DUMP AND DONE RAMEN SALAD

3 (3-ounce) packages chicken-flavored ramen

1 (12-ounce) package broccoli slaw

1 cup thinly sliced red onion

1 cup frozen peas

¾ cup corn kernels (fresh, frozen, or canned—but c'mon, it's got to be canned)

½ cup sugar

⅓ cup vegetable oil

½ cup apple cider vinegar

1 cup roasted, salted sunflower seeds

Nothing in this book makes me laugh harder than this recipe. I was drinking a whiskey at my sister's baby shower in Cedar Falls, Iowa, awaiting the arrival of Jell-O salad, cheesy potatoes, BBQ chicken, the family-gathering favorites. Little did I know that when I reached the end of the buffet line, I would be greeted by a magical delight called *ramen salad*. I swear it had a glow and a halo. I shoved everything else to the side. I have never been so excited to re-create something in my life. It's like Cup Noodles on acid. It IS Cup Noodles IN acid. The only way the crushed-up ramen noodles and veggies "cook" is in the vinegar dressing. And you use the packet of seasoning!!! I CAN'T EXPRESS HOW HAPPY THIS SALAD MAKES ME. Your friends will laugh, oh yes, they'll laugh. But I haven't met a single human who could stop eating this. BON APPÉTIT, MES AMOURS, and thank you, Aunt Debby, for introducing me to a dish that clearly makes me extremely emotionally fired up.

Set the seasoning packets from the ramen aside. Crush the ramen noodles into a salad bowl, then add the slaw, onion, peas, and corn and toss.

In a microwave-safe bowl, combine the sugar, oil, vinegar, and ramen seasoning packets and microwave on high for 1 minute. Pour the hot dressing over the slaw mixture and toss. Refrigerate for 3 hours or overnight.

Toss in the sunflower seeds just before serving.

NOODLES AND CARBS

// *Opposite:* Pepper's Scalloped Potatoes (PAGE 94)

SERVES 4

PREP TIME: 10 minutes **TOTAL TIME:** 25 minutes

LEMONY ARUGULA SPAGHETTI CACIO E PEPE

Kosher salt

12 ounces dried spaghetti

¼ pound pancetta or bacon, finely diced (about ¾ cup)

¼ cup extra-virgin olive oil

3 tablespoons minced garlic (about 4 big cloves)

1 teaspoon red pepper flakes, plus more to taste

2 teaspoons freshly ground black pepper, plus more to taste

¼ cup fresh lemon juice

1½ cups freshly grated Parmigiano-Reggiano cheese, plus more for serving

3 cups baby arugula

Some say love conquers all, but I say *cacio e pepe* does. It's true, John and I fell for each other *and* got married in Lake Como, Italy, but it's also where I became a slave to this pasta dish, which is super peppery and cheesy and is basically the boss of me whenever I make it. At first I was a little worried: Since I first tasted it when I was all gooey-romancey in Italia, would it weather the trip home? DID I HAVE PASTA GOGGLES ON? Thankfully, I adore it as much now as I did then—even more, actually. Which is a good thing to be able to say about pasta recipes as well as husbands.

In a large pot of heavily salted boiling water, cook the spaghetti to al dente according to the package directions. Reserve 1 cup of the pasta water (it comes in handy), then drain the pasta.

Meanwhile, in a large skillet, cook the pancetta over medium-high heat until crisped, 7 to 9 minutes. Add the olive oil, then add the garlic, red pepper flakes, and black pepper and cook until fragrant, about 1 minute.

Add the lemon juice to the skillet, then toss in the drained pasta and toss to coat. Add the Parm and toss, adding the pasta water, a couple of tablespoons at a time, just to help the cheese coat the pasta. Add the arugula and toss until it wilts, about 1 minute. Season to taste with additional salt, lots of black pepper, and red pepper flakes. Serve with more Parm.

SERVES 8 TO 10

PREP TIME: 20 minutes **TOTAL TIME:** 1 hour 30 minutes

BAKED PASTA ALLA NORMA
WITH MOZZARELLA BOMBS

for the **EGGPLANT**

- 1 cup olive oil (a lot, yes, but necessary)
- 2½ pounds eggplant, peeled and cut into 1-inch cubes
- 1 tablespoon kosher salt
- 1 teaspoon freshly ground black pepper
- 2 teaspoons red pepper flakes

for the **ZITI**

- Kosher salt
- 1 pound ziti or penne pasta (preferably with ridges)
- Perfect Tomato Sauce (recipe follows)
- 2 cups (about 15 ounces) whole-milk ricotta cheese
- 1½ pounds fresh mozzarella (I like buffalo), cut into ¾-inch cubes
- 1 cup (lightly packed) basil leaves, torn by hand
- 1 teaspoon freshly ground black pepper
- 1 teaspoon red pepper flakes

I used to think the secret to great eggplant was to salt it and gently oven-roast it, but then Norma showed up in my life and properly schooled me. She taught me that a cup of olive oil needs to be sacrificed in the name of the tender, melt-in-your-mouth eggplant that goes into this crusty, cheesy, tomato-saucey baked pasta dish. Oh, and sorry, you have to use fresh mozzarella because Norma says so. So listen to Norma, because she's one smart bitch, and you'll get seconds if you don't talk back.

COOK THE EGGPLANT: In a large skillet or a wide soup pot, heat the oil over medium-high heat. When you can see little waves in the oil, carefully add the eggplant, and sprinkle on the salt, black pepper, and red pepper flakes and cook, stirring once in a while, until the eggplant is soft and golden brown, 15 to 20 minutes. Remove from the heat and let cool slightly.

MAKE AND BAKE THE ZITI: While the eggplant is cooking, in a large pot of salted boiling water, cook the ziti to al dente according to the package directions. Drain and transfer to a large bowl.

Preheat the oven to 400°F.

Add the eggplant (and any oil from the skillet) to the pasta along with the tomato sauce, ricotta, two thirds of the mozzarella, the basil, 1½ teaspoons salt, the black pepper, and red pepper flakes. Dump the mixture into a large baking dish and top with the rest of the mozzarella, gently pressing the pieces into the pasta.

Bake until golden and bubbling, about 1 hour. Let stand for 5 minutes before serving.

perfect tomato sauce

MAKES 6 CUPS

PREP TIME: 5 minutes
TOTAL TIME: 50 minutes

½ cup extra-virgin olive oil
2 cups diced onions (about 2 medium)
2 tablespoons finely minced garlic (about 4 cloves)
3½ pounds juicy, ripe Roma (plum) tomatoes, diced, or 1 (28-ounce) can diced tomatoes plus 1 (28-ounce) can crushed tomatoes
2 tablespoons chopped fresh oregano
2 tablespoons chopped fresh thyme
1 tablespoon chopped fresh rosemary
1 teaspoon kosher salt
½ teaspoon freshly ground black pepper

In a 4-quart saucepan, heat the oil over medium heat. Add the onions and cook, stirring, until translucent and beginning to turn golden, about 13 minutes. Add the garlic and cook until fragrant, 1 minute longer. Add the tomatoes, oregano, thyme, rosemary, salt, and pepper. Bring to a boil, then reduce to a simmer and cook until the sauce thickens slightly, 25 to 30 minutes for fresh tomatoes, 20 to 25 minutes for canned.

SERVES 4 TO 6

PREP TIME: 10 minutes **TOTAL TIME:** 35 minutes

SWEET AND SALTY COCONUT RICE

½ cup unsweetened shredded coconut

1½ cups jasmine rice, rinsed and drained

1 (14-ounce) can coconut milk (full-fat, not light)

¼ cup sugar

1½ teaspoons kosher salt

There are a million foods I love. But I can EVENTUALLY get full off fried chicken. I can EVENTUALLY fill up on mac and cheese. But I for real cannot stop myself from eating this until every grain of rice in the immediate vicinity has been consumed. My plate, other plates, sides of the pot it was cooked in. Did any fall on the floor? That is now mine. Someone get up to go to the bathroom? Your rice is now mine. Too engaged in conversation to watch your plate? Mine.

There is just an incredible amount of stuff this dish can go with in this book but ohhhhh my god: a scoop or nine under the Pineapple-Grilled Short Ribs (page 194) makes my weak heart pitter-patter.

If you aren't sold from that pitch, you need a therapist. You can see mine; she's great, kinda pricey, but she is also a dog.*

** If you know my dogs and you're wondering, it's Puddy. Pippa doesn't care about your issues. Penny has her own. Puddy just floats through life.*

In a dry skillet, toast the coconut over medium-low heat, stirring, until lightly browned and fragrant, 4 to 5 minutes. Transfer to a plate to cool (if you leave it in the skillet it might burn).

In a medium saucepan, combine the rice, coconut milk, 1¾ cups water (1 empty coconut milk can full!), sugar, and salt and bring to a boil over high heat, stirring occasionally. Reduce the heat to a barely bubbling simmer, cover, and simmer until the rice is cooked and the liquid is absorbed (there may be a bubbly layer of coconut cream on top of the cooked rice, so poke through it to make sure the rice is cooked), about 20 minutes. Remove from the heat and fluff with a fork, re-cover the saucepan, and let stand for 5 minutes.

Transfer to a serving bowl and top with the toasted coconut.

SERVES 4

PREP TIME: 10 minutes **TOTAL TIME:** 20 minutes

PEPPER'S SPICY CLAMS AND PASTA

My mom Pepper's only goals in life are to (1) be an Instagram star, (2) do everything humanly possible to take care of me on a daily basis no matter how old I get (love you, Mom!), and (3) find Manila clams. I'm not kidding. This woman has clams on the brain 23/7 (she only sleeps for an hour a day and I suspect that even then, she is still dreaming of clams).

When I told her that hey, maybe you guys wouldn't want to just sit and munch on pounds of clams on their own like she does, she was more than willing to toss it up into my absolute favorite way to eat pasta: linguine alle vongole with a kick of red pepper flakes. Her garlic and butter clams + my spicy love for Italy. Mama mia/mama and me-ahahahaahah; I give up.

- Kosher salt
- 12 ounces dried linguine
- 1 stick (4 ounces) unsalted butter
- 2 tablespoons extra-virgin olive oil
- 8 cloves garlic, minced
- 1 teaspoon red pepper flakes
- ½ cup dry white wine
- ¼ teaspoon freshly ground black pepper
- 2 pounds Manila clams, scrubbed
- ½ cup chopped fresh parsley, plus more for garnish

In a large pot of heavily salted boiling water, cook the linguine until al dente according to the package directions. Reserve ¼ cup of the pasta water, then drain the pasta and return it to the cooking pot.

Meanwhile, in a large skillet, heat the butter and olive oil over medium heat. When the butter foams, add the garlic and red pepper flakes and cook until the garlic is fragrant and very lightly golden, 2 to 3 minutes. Add the wine and pepper, increase the heat slightly, and cook until bubbling, about 2 minutes. Add the clams, increase the heat, cover, and cook just until the clams open, about 3 minutes. Transfer the opened clams to the pasta pot. (If some clams are stubborn, re-cover the pan for another minute or two; if the clams still don't open, ditch them.) Taste the sauce and add salt to taste.

Add any remaining cooked clams and all the clam liquid to the drained pasta. Warm through over medium heat, adding the reserved pasta water as needed to help bind the sauce.

Toss in the parsley, divide the pasta and clams among bowls, and garnish with more parsley if you want.

de-sand yo' clams

Sometimes clams have sand. You want no sand. So, first of all, see if there are any already opened clams. Tap on them; if they don't try to close back up, toss them and let them rest in peace. Place the totally-sealed-shut clams in a bowl and cover with cold water. Let them sit for 20 minutes. You'll see some sand in the bowl after they sit. Then carefully lift them out of the bowl and scrub all over their shells, especially the hinge, with a clean, stiff brush under running water to remove any extra grit.

SERVES 6

PREP TIME: 15 minutes **TOTAL TIME:** 35 minutes

ACTUAL DRUNKEN NOODLES

for the **SAUCE**

- 6 tablespoons light brown sugar
- ½ cup soy sauce (regular, not light)
- ¼ cup oyster sauce
- 2 tablespoons whiskey
- 1 tablespoon mirin
- 1 tablespoon sambal oelek, or other chile sauce
- 1 tablespoon chopped garlic

for the **STIR-FRY**

- 4 tablespoons canola oil
- 4 eggs, beaten
- 1¼ pounds boneless, skinless chicken breasts, cut into ½-inch cubes
- 1 teaspoon sesame oil
- ½ teaspoon kosher salt
- 4 scallions, thinly sliced, plus more for garnish
- 2 tablespoons minced fresh ginger
- 2 tablespoons minced garlic (about 4 cloves)
- 4 cups broccoli florets
- 2 cups white mushrooms, thinly sliced
- ½ cup low-sodium chicken broth
- 12 ounces dried wide rice noodles (softened according to package directions) or 1½ pounds fresh wide rice noodles

The funny thing about drunken noodles is that none of the recipes I've ever found actually have alcohol in them—you are supposed to eat them WHILE drunk as a hangover cure (I am not opposed), but I decided they'd be good actually drunk themselves, so I added whiskey. The noodles are big, flat sponges for the sauce, and there's broccoli for John, plus scrambled eggs and chicken, and you can (should) hit it with some really spicy sh*t. Pepper gave me major side-eye when she caught me developing this Thai-ish recipe without her permission, but she actually ate a whole bowlful. So I win.

MAKE THE SAUCE: In a bowl, combine the brown sugar, soy sauce, oyster sauce, whiskey, mirin, sambal, and garlic. Set aside.

MAKE THE STIR-FRY: In a wok or a really big skillet, heat 1 tablespoon of the canola oil over medium-high heat. Pour in the eggs and cook, stirring, until the eggs form large curds. Transfer to a medium bowl and cover to keep warm. Wipe out or clean the pan if you need to get any stuck egg out.

Toss the chicken breast with the sesame oil and salt. Heat another 1 tablespoon of the canola oil in the wok over high heat, until it smokes, add the chicken, and stir-fry until just cooked through and no longer pink, 4 to 5 minutes. Transfer to the bowl with the eggs and cover.

Add the remaining 2 tablespoons oil to the pan over high heat. When it smokes, add the scallions, ginger, and garlic and cook, stirring, until fragrant and the scallions are bright green, 20 seconds. Add the broccoli, mushrooms, and broth and cook, stirring, until the broccoli turns bright green and the stock is almost evaporated, 2 to 3 minutes. Add the noodles, chicken and eggs, and the sauce to the wok. Cook, tossing the mixture, until warmed though, the noodles are cooked, and the sauce at the bottom of the wok bubbles and thickens, 4 to 5 minutes. Garnish with scallions.

sambalism

I know I use a lot of Sriracha, but sometimes I use sambal oelek instead for a similar but not-the-same effect. Unlike Sriracha, which has some sweetness and tang thanks to sugar and vinegar, this is basically smashed-up chiles with some salt and garlic thrown in for good measure. It's hot, but not death-hot, and it's delicious.

SERVES 4 AS A LIGHT MEAL or 6 AS A SIDE DISH

PREP TIME: 15 minutes **TOTAL TIME:** 45 minutes

SESAME CHICKEN NOODLES

If you can pronounce tahini (it's ta-HEE-nee, rhymes with bikini), you can make these noodles. OK, even if you can't, you'll ace them, because few things in this book are so good and so frigging easy. There's even a magic chicken breast that you cook in hot water off the flame. Then you cook the pasta in the same water before you coat the cold pasta in a sticky, nutty dressing and realize you can pull off this dish smoothly without taking a Xanax.

Kosher salt

1 (8-ounce) boneless, skinless chicken breast

8 ounces dried fettuccine

2 teaspoons sesame oil

¼ cup peanut oil

¼ cup tahini

3 tablespoons soy sauce

2 tablespoons red wine vinegar

2 teaspoons chili oil

1 teaspoon honey

½ teaspoon cayenne pepper

1 garlic clove, minced

2 scallions, thinly sliced

Fill a large saucepan two-thirds full of water and bring to a boil over high heat. Salt it so that it tastes good, add the chicken breast, and remove the pot from the heat. Cover and let the chicken sit until cooked but very tender, about 15 minutes. (If you're using 2 smaller breasts, decrease the time by about 3 minutes.) Remove the chicken from the water (don't throw the water away! You'll see why in a minute) and cut into it to check its doneness; if it's still a little pink, return it to the water for another minute or two. Remove the chicken to a plate and let it rest while you cook the noodles.

Bring the water the chicken was cooked in back to a boil over high heat. Add the fettuccine and cook to al dente according to the package directions. Drain, rinse the pasta in cold water until cool, then shake it dry in a colander.

While the pasta cooks, in a medium bowl, whisk together 1 teaspoon of the sesame oil, the peanut oil, tahini, soy sauce, vinegar, chili oil, honey, cayenne, and garlic until smooth.

Transfer the noodles to a large bowl and use a clean paper towel to gently pat the noodles as dry as is actually reasonable. Toss the noodles with the remaining 1 teaspoon sesame oil.

Shred the chicken with your hands or chop it into bite-size pieces and add it to the noodles. Add the dressing and toss to coat. Garnish with the scallions.

SERVES 8 TO 12

PREP TIME: 45 minutes **TOTAL TIME:** 1 hour

CHRISSY'S MAC AND CHEESE

WITH CHEESY GARLIC BREAD CRUMBS

This is MY mac and cheese, dammit. Everyone is allllllways asking, begging John to make his mac and cheese and if I may be frank here for a moment: I DON'T GET IT.

I will admit, I like it too, but I prefer a creamy, saucy mac. Mac and cheese that you give your friends to take home in Tupperware, not sliced and wrapped in foil like a brick.

OK, so maybe I'm bitter. Every single time he makes his mac and cheese, people lose it, like he literally invented mac and cheese. Why? It's because he is a brilliant, handsome, kind, wonderful f*cking human being who is incredibly talented and famous who *happens* to make a good mac and cheese. It's *one more talent and whoa we did not see this coming.* AMAZE.

I'm sorry, John. I love you so, so much and you are absolutely perfect. My dream man. You write songs about me, love me endlessly, you clean, you help me unpack, and you are a wonderful dog father.

But my mac is better. If you want to try his, google it. These pages are expensive.

Kosher salt
1 pound pasta shells
1 teaspoon vegetable oil
1 stick (4 ounces) unsalted butter, plus more for greasing the baking dish
5 tablespoons all-purpose flour
5 cups whole milk
3 cups grated cheddar cheese
3 cups grated Gruyère or Swiss cheese
¾ pound orange American cheese (about 16 slices)
Freshly ground black pepper
¾ teaspoon cayenne pepper, or more to taste
Cheesy Garlic Bread Crumbs (recipe follows)

Preheat the oven to 425°F.

In a large pot of salted boiling water, cook the pasta a minute less than called for on the package. Drain, rinse, and toss with the oil to prevent sticking.

Grease a 9 × 13-inch baking dish with a little butter.

In a large saucepan or soup pot, heat the 1 stick butter over medium-high heat until melted but not browning. Add the flour and cook, constantly whisking, until it turns a light and toasty brown color, 5 to 6 minutes. Gradually add the milk while whisking, then increase the heat and bring it to a boil. Reduce the heat to medium and cook, whisking, until it thickens, 4 to 5 minutes. Add the cheeses, a few handfuls/slices at a time, reserving a handful of the cheese, and whisk the sauce until smooth. Whisk in 2 teaspoons salt, ¼ teaspoon black pepper, and the cayenne.

Stir in the cooked pasta, season to taste with more salt and pepper, and cook until the pasta is hot again.

Pour the mixture into the buttered baking dish. Top with the remaining cheese and spread the bread crumbs evenly over the top. Bake until the topping is browned and crisp, about 8 minutes.

cheesy garlic bread crumbs

MAKES ABOUT 4 CUPS

PREP TIME: 5 minutes **TOTAL TIME:** 25 minutes

8 slices white sandwich bread, torn into pieces
6 cloves garlic
6 tablespoons unsalted butter
1 teaspoon kosher salt
½ teaspoon freshly ground black pepper
5 tablespoons finely grated Parmigiano-Reggiano

In a food processor, process the bread until it forms fine crumbs (you should have about 4 cups crumbs). Transfer the crumbs to a bowl. Add the garlic to the processor and process until finely minced (or do it by hand).

In a large skillet, heat the butter over medium-low heat. When it foams, add the garlic and cook, stirring, until the garlic smells great but hasn't browned, 1 to 2 minutes. Add the bread crumbs, increase the heat to medium, and cook, stirring frequently, until toasty and browned, 7 to 9 minutes. Stir in the salt and pepper, remove from the heat, and transfer to a large plate to cool for 5 minutes. Toss in the Parm.

SERVES 6 TO 8

PREP TIME: 20 minutes **TOTAL TIME:** 1 hour

CHEESY JALAPEÑO BACON CORNBREAD

- 6 slices bacon
- 1 stick (4 ounces) unsalted butter, cut into chunks
- 1 cup canned cream-style corn
- ¾ cup buttermilk, shaken
- 3 large eggs, beaten
- 1 cup shredded cheddar cheese
- ½ cup finely grated Parmigiano-Reggiano cheese
- ½ cup sliced pickled jalapeño peppers, chopped
- 1½ cups cornmeal
- 2 teaspoons sugar
- 1½ teaspoons baking soda
- 1½ teaspoons kosher salt
- 1 teaspoon freshly ground black pepper

We all know those people who are super stuck in their ways because, well, nostalgia. I'm like this with stuffing. I truly don't believe there is a better stuffing out there than Stove Top. I've had it all: The apples. The walnuts. The sausage. Allllllll your fancy little ways. Nothing ever makes me happier than Stove Top in all its herby, MSG goodness.

John is like this with cornbread. For him, nothing will ever top his box of Jiffy. But oh, I was willing to accept this challenge. Let's just say we are now a Jiffy-free household.

Preheat the oven to 375°F

In a 10-inch cast-iron skillet, cook the bacon over medium heat, turning occasionally, until crisp, about 9 minutes. Transfer the bacon to paper towels to drain, leaving the bacon fat in the skillet. When cool, crumble the bacon.

Add the butter to the hot bacon fat to melt, then pour it into a large bowl and let cool for 10 minutes. (Don't wipe out the skillet.) Stir the creamed corn into the melted fats, then add the buttermilk, eggs, cheeses, jalapeños, and crumbled bacon.

In another large bowl, combine the cornmeal, sugar, baking soda, salt, and pepper. Add the wet ingredients to the dry and stir until incorporated. Pour the batter into the skillet and bake until the top is lightly browned and the center is set, 30 to 35 minutes.

Let the cornbread cool slightly before slicing.

SERVES A SH*T-TON OF PEOPLE (16 TO 20)

PREP TIME: 45 minutes **TOTAL TIME:** 3 hours

PEPPER'S SCALLOPED POTATOES

"What would your death row meal be?" is the most popular question I'm asked, just ahead of "DOEs HE SInG 2 U????"

I love this question because (1) the asker assumes I will one day be on death row, so they get me and (2) it's the easiest question on the planet—it is this dish. This creamy creation, which my mom has been making my entire life, puts me into a state of instant euphoria and you can't go a single bite without a bacon or ham bomb.

I was notorious for sneaking undercooked scoops from the edges of the pan, not being able to control these potato-y desires of mine. By the time mom removed it from the oven, the edges were completely gone, leaving behind just a giant dollop of potato, balancing in the middle of the casserole dish.

And my god, the leftovers. I should add Tupperware to the list of ingredients because I can't tell you how many times I've put a few servings of this in my purse for a flight. If you make one thing in this book, make this, I beg you. (See photograph, page 76.)

5 pounds russet (Idaho) potatoes

1 medium onion, finely chopped

1⅓ pounds ham, cut into ½-inch cubes

8 slices bacon (not thick-cut), cut into squares

1 stick (4 ounces) unsalted butter

2 tablespoons garlic salt

½ teaspoon freshly ground black pepper

1½ cups all-purpose flour

5½ cups whole milk

Preheat the oven to 375°F.

Peel the potatoes, halve them lengthwise, and slice them crosswise into thin half-moons. Rinse well with cold water and drain in a colander. Transfer the potatoes to a large bowl and toss them with the onion and the ham.

In a large Dutch oven, cook half the bacon over medium-low heat until the fat is rendered and the bacon is crispy, 9 to 10 minutes. Add the butter and cook, stirring, until melted, making sure the butter doesn't burn. Add the garlic salt and pepper, then whisk in the flour and cook, stirring to work out the lumps, until smooth. Whisk in the milk until smooth. Increase the heat to high and bring to a boil. Cook, whisking, until thickened, about 5 minutes. Transfer the sauce to a bowl.

Arrange half the potato mixture in the bottom of the Dutch oven, then cover it with half the sauce. Repeat with the remaining potatoes and sauce. Arrange the uncooked bacon squares on top of the sauce and bake, uncovered, until the bacon appears crispy and rendered, 30 to 35 minutes. Reduce the oven temperature to 350°F, cover with the lid, and cook until bubbling, 1 hour 30 minutes longer.

SERVES 8 TO 10

PREP TIME: 30 minutes **TOTAL TIME:** 1 hour 15 minutes

CREAMY POTATO SALAD
WITH BACON

How do people hate mayo? They will toss eggs down their gullet, consume oil by the pound, but heaven forbid we mix the two together. I promise you, this will make everyone forget about their prized vinegar-based potato salad. If I can't turn you on with the words "creamy potato with bacon," I give up.

- **4 pounds medium red potatoes**
- **Kosher salt**
- **12 ounces bacon**
- **1½ cups mayonnaise**
- **3 tablespoons Dijon mustard**
- **2 heaping tablespoons sweet pickle relish**
- **A squeeze of yellow mustard**
- **½ teaspoon freshly ground black pepper**
- **4 hard-boiled eggs (see Note), chopped**
- **½ cup finely diced red onion**
- **¼ cup thinly sliced scallion greens**
- **1 large jalapeño pepper, seeded and finely diced**

In a large pot, combine the potatoes with water to cover. Salt it until it tastes good, and bring to a boil over high heat. Reduce the heat to a simmer and cook until you can pierce the potatoes easily with a fork, 20 to 25 minutes. Drain and cool to room temperature, then cut them into bite-size pieces and transfer to a large bowl.

Cut the bacon into ¼-inch pieces. In a medium skillet, cook half the bacon over medium heat until crispy, about 10 minutes. Drain on paper towels. Repeat with the remaining bacon.

In a small bowl, whisk together the mayo, Dijon mustard, relish, yellow mustard, black pepper, and 2 teaspoons salt until smooth.

Add the dressing to the potatoes along with the bacon, eggs, onion, scallion greens, and jalapeño. Gently toss to combine.

note // See Secretly Spicy Deviled Eggs (page 132) for my favorite method of cooking hard-boiled eggs.

SERVES 6

PREP TIME: 10 minutes **TOTAL TIME:** 35 minutes

SMASHED POTATOES
WITH ROASTED GARLIC

- 2½ pounds baby red potatoes
- Kosher salt
- 1 stick (4 ounces) butter
- ½ cup heavy cream
- ½ teaspoon freshly ground black pepper
- 15 large cloves (½ cup packed) Roasted Garlic (page 163)
- 2 tablespoons chopped chives

Here's something I bet you don't know about me: I lived in Idaho for a good amount of my childhood and it. Was. Awesome. I had a pot-bellied pig named Junior, who slept in a baby playpen until he chewed his way through it one night. Mom painted his toenails red and he would squeal any chance he got. He was pure chaos, and we loved it.

I forget where this was going.

Oh! Potatoes. Washington's abundance of salmon makes me cringe at smoked salmon to this day, but somehow living in Idaho only made me want potatoes more. I mean I actually ate *potato ice cream*. That is a thing there. A thing I did every single weekend.

My spud-loving palate and my Idaho roots know only the best potato dishes, and sometimes things are best done simply. This = one of those things.

In a large pot, combine the potatoes with cold water to cover them by 3 inches. Salt the water until it tastes good. Bring the pot to a boil over high heat, reduce the heat to a simmer, and cook the potatoes until you can pierce them easily with a fork, about 25 minutes.

Meanwhile, in a small saucepan, heat the butter, cream, pepper, and 1½ teaspoons salt and keep it warm over low heat.

Drain the potatoes, return them to the pot, and add the roasted garlic. Using a potato masher or potato ricer, mash until chunky-smooth, then stir in the warmed cream mixture. Transfer to a serving bowl and sprinkle with the chives.

SERVES 6 TO 8

PREP TIME: 35 minutes **TOTAL TIME:** 1 hour

SOUR CREAM AND BROCCOLI BAKED POTATO CAKES

These take me back to the days when Mom had to sneak veggies into our diets any which way she could. JK, she didn't give a sh*t about whether or not we ate our vegetables because hello, it's time for *A Current Affair*! Pep was casual like that. Plus my sister and I were human garbage disposals who did not discriminate when it came to food, green or not.

These are an adult Chrissy treat. Serve a hot plate of them with a family-style meal and it will be the first thing people's hands launch to grab.

- **3 cups broccoli florets**
- **Kosher salt**
- **1½ pounds russet (Idaho) potatoes**
- **1 cup finely grated Parmigiano-Reggiano cheese**
- **1 cup sour cream, plus more for serving**
- **1 egg, beaten**
- **½ teaspoon freshly ground black pepper**
- **4 tablespoons canola oil**
- **1 tablespoon butter**
- **2 tablespoons chopped chives, for serving**

Place the broccoli in a single layer in a microwave-safe dish and add ½ inch water and a few pinches of salt. Cover. Microwave the broccoli on high until it turns bright green, about 3 minutes. Remove the broccoli, drain, and cool on paper towels to absorb any extra moisture.

Pierce the potatoes all over with a fork, then wrap each potato in a damp paper towel. Place the potatoes on a microwave-safe plate and microwave on high until soft, about 15 minutes.

Remove from the microwave, cool slightly, then halve the potatoes and use a fork to scrape the flesh from the potatoes into a bowl. Leave the skins behind and mash the flesh until smooth, then mix in the broccoli, Parm, sour cream, egg, pepper, and 1½ teaspoons salt. Form the mixture into twelve 3-inch round patties.

Preheat the oven to 250°F.

In a large skillet, heat 2 tablespoons of the oil and ½ tablespoon of the butter over medium-high heat. When the butter foams, add 6 patties and pan-fry until golden, 3 to 4 minutes per side. Drain briefly on paper towels and keep warm in the oven on a baking sheet. Repeat with the remaining oil, butter, and patties.

Serve the potato cakes with more sour cream and the chives.

From left: Smashed Potatoes with Roasted Garlic (PAGE 98), John's Crispy Roasted Potatoes (PAGE 102), Hasselback Potatoes (PAGE 103), Sour Cream and Broccoli Baked Potato Cakes (PAGE 99)

SERVES 4 TO 6

PREP TIME: 15 minutes **TOTAL TIME:** 1 hour

JOHN'S CRISPY ROASTED POTATOES

Roasted potatoes usually don't stand a chance. I mean, if you had to choose between a French fry, a tater tot, a potato chip, and a sad little mushy roasted potato, what would you do? (Don't worry, me too.) But John really loves them, so I was determined to make them good enough that I don't pick up a magazine in the supermarket one day and read that he's left me for a nanny with a culinary degree and a specialty in spuds.

The secret is to preheat the oil in the baking sheet (get one with rims, people, or your oven will become one giant grease fire) so when the potatoes touch it they get a crispy contact high. DFWT!!! Don't. F*ck. With. Them. Every time you stir them (which you will be tempted to do) you sacrifice some of those edges and crunchy bits. So put the potatoes in the oven and then paint your nails or handcuff yourself or do something, anything, that will prevent you from messing up these salty, crunchy, golden-brown spuds.

- **5 tablespoons extra-virgin olive oil**
- **1½ pounds red or russet (Idaho) potatoes, cut into 1-inch wedges**
- **1 medium onion, halved and cut into ½-inch wedges**
- **4 cloves garlic**
- **4 rosemary sprigs**
- **Kosher salt and freshly ground black pepper**

Preheat the oven to 425°F. Pour 4 tablespoons of the oil onto a rimmed baking sheet and heat in the oven until very hot but not smoking, about 10 minutes.

In a large bowl, toss the remaining 1 tablespoon oil with the potatoes, onion, garlic, rosemary, and 1½ teaspoons each salt and pepper. Remove the baking sheet with the heated oil and immediately but carefully pour the potato mixture onto the sheet, spread out in a single layer, and return to the oven. Roast the potatoes until the undersides are crisped and the garlic begins to soften, 20 to 25 minutes. Remove the baking sheet from the oven and flip the potatoes using a metal spatula (or, if you're John, one by one with tongs). Return the potatoes to the oven and roast until the garlic is golden and softened and the potatoes are crisped but tender when poked with a fork, 15 to 20 minutes longer. Season to taste with more salt and pepper.

SERVES 4

PREP TIME: 15 minutes **TOTAL TIME:** 1 hour 30 minutes

HASSELBACK POTATOES

- 4 medium russet (Idaho) potatoes (1½ pounds)
- 6 tablespoons butter, melted
- ⅓ cup olive oil
- 2 tablespoons chopped fresh thyme
- 1½ teaspoons kosher salt
- ½ teaspoon freshly ground black pepper, plus more to taste
- ¼ cup finely grated Parmigiano-Reggiano cheese

special **EQUIPMENT** A pair of chopsticks

Want to waste three hours of your life like I did? Do a google image search of these potatoes. You've never seen so many beautiful, armadillo-looking potatoes in your life. They are legit 200 percent more photogenic than I am. It's like each potato went to Glamour Shots and instead of feather boas, star glasses, and silk gloves, their props are bacon crumbles, cheddar cheese, herbs, and sour cream.

We keep our Hasselback potatoes relatively simple but the world is your tater! I can't imagine what could not go inside these little spud slots, aside from beets because beets are the devil's root.

Actually, I just googled hasselback beets and it's a thing. We're doomed.

Preheat the oven to 400°F.

Lay a potato on a cutting board with a long side facing you. Place a chopstick on either side of the potato. Using a sharp knife, slice the potato crosswise into ⅛-inch slices, using the chopsticks as a stopper so you don't cut all the way through the potato. (Using chopsticks to help out the potatoes is like East and West coming together in peace and harmony.) Repeat with the remaining potatoes.

Arrange the potatoes on a rimmed baking sheet. In a small bowl, mix together the melted butter, oil, and thyme. Drizzle the potatoes with half of the oil-butter mixture, separating the potato slices slightly so it drips down into the crevices. Season with the salt and pepper. Bake until the potatoes start to soften, 30 to 35 minutes. Remove from the oven, drizzle with the remaining butter-oil mixture, then return to the oven to bake until the potato edges get browned and crisp, 30 to 35 minutes longer. Remove from the oven and dust each potato generously with the Parm.

THAI MOM

// *Opposite:* Pepper's Thai Beef Salad (PAGE 106)

SERVES 6

PREP TIME: 25 minutes **TOTAL TIME:** 35 minutes

PEPPER'S THAI BEEF SALAD

for the **BEEF**

- 2 well-marbled New York strip or boneless rib-eye steaks (1 inch thick, 1¾ pounds total)
- Freshly ground black pepper
- 3 tablespoons light soy sauce
- 2 tablespoons vegetable oil

for the **DRESSING AND SALAD**

- 3 tablespoons fresh lime juice
- 3 tablespoons fish sauce
- 2 teaspoons ground Thai chili powder (see Note, opposite) or 1 teaspoon cayenne pepper
- 2 tablespoons Toasted Rice (recipe follows)
- 6 fresh mint leaves, sliced
- ½ cup chopped fresh cilantro leaves
- 2 scallions, thinly sliced
- 10 grape tomatoes, halved
- Pepper's Red Hot Pepper Sauce (recipe follows; optional), for serving
- Steamed rice, for serving (optional)

Remember in school when you would have potlucks? Before the days of TIMMY CAN'T BE WITHIN 6 MILES OF A PEANUT? My mom used to send me with this Thai beef salad, which, as you can imagine, really stood out in a sea of mac and cheese and dinosaur-shaped chicken tenders. Although I was kind of embarrassed the first few times to unwrap this oddball dish, people really loved it and looked forward to it every damn quarter. Make sure to get well-marbled meat and not to overcook the steak—the acid in the dressing will "cook" it even more. It should be pretty rare but sure, overcook it if you want. Just don't tell me about it. (See photograph, page 104.)

COOK THE BEEF: Season the steaks generously with black pepper and roll in the soy sauce to coat.

In a cast-iron skillet, heat the oil over high heat until smoking. Add the steaks (one at a time if they both won't fit comfortably in your skillet) and sear until medium-rare, 4 to 5 minutes per side. Remove to a plate, let rest for 10 minutes, then thinly slice against the grain.

MAKE THE DRESSING AND SALAD: In a large bowl, combine the lime juice, fish sauce, and chili powder. Add the beef, toasted rice, mint, cilantro, scallions, and tomatoes and toss to coat. Serve immediately, with hot pepper sauce and steamed rice if you want.

toasted rice

MAKES ABOUT ¼ CUP

PREP TIME: 15 minutes

TOTAL TIME: 20 minutes

This is a thing in Thai cooking—you toast up a bunch of raw rice, pulverize it, and sprinkle it on things for crunch and nuttiness. God, I love Thai people. Sometimes they have these super thrifty flavor tricks, and sometimes they're literally just like "OK, this dish is good and all, but how do we incorporate chunks of fat?" This is a sentence I can get down with.

½ cup jasmine rice

In a dry heavy skillet, toast the rice over medium heat, stirring and tossing often and watching closely so it doesn't burn, until deep brown, 12 to 14 minutes. Transfer to a plate to cool completely, then pound in a mortar and pestle to a powder the consistency of fine bread crumbs (or blend in a blender on high speed for 10 to 15 seconds; make sure you've dried the blender well). Store the rice in an airtight container for when your Thai Mom comes calling.

pepper's red hot pepper sauce

MAKES ½ CUP

TOTAL TIME: 10 minutes

If you want to jack up this salad (or any dish that needs a jolt of Thai-style heat), make my mom's sickly delicious sauce, which keeps in the fridge forever.

2 tablespoons ground Thai chili powder
2 tablespoons hot water
2 tablespoons fish sauce
1 tablespoon Toasted Rice (above)
10 grape tomatoes, halved

In a small bowl, combine the chili powder and hot water. Stir in the fish sauce and toasted rice. Squeeze in the pulp of the tomatoes (discard the skins) and stir.

homemade thai chili powder

Mom makes her own chili powder from red Thai bird chiles she dries in our backyard. But if you want to make the chili powder, buy dried Thai chiles (available at Thai markets) or dried serrano chiles (available at Mexican markets) and grind them up in a spice grinder or with a mortar and pestle until fine. It lasts indefinitely in a sealed container at room temp.

SERVES 8

PREP TIME: 15 minutes **TOTAL TIME:** 1 hour

JOK MOO (THAI PORK AND RICE PORRIDGE)

I feel like I have lived a million lives—the things I get to see, the people I get to meet. There is no word that describes it more than "blessed." But there are certain moments that stick out more than others, one being the time I made my mom's pork and rice porridge for Eric Ripert, one of the best chefs in the world, and who also happens to be a wonderfully kind and generous man. Seeing him eat it, and love it, actually brought me to tears. (Apparently even the most cynical harbor the water necessary to produce tears.)

Mom has been making this since before I can remember. It's so simple: garlicky chunks of peppery ground pork and fresh ginger in a thick rice broth. It's the ultimate comfort food when I'm feeling down, the perfect cure for a hangover. Violently ill? You'll keep this down. Been stabbed? Apply to the wound. Headache? Put in a Ziploc and apply to forehead. I really believe that there is nothing this soup can't cure.

By the way, *moo* is Thai for "pork." Don't get me started on why beef isn't *oink*, lamb isn't *bokbok,* and chicken isn't *baa*.

1½ cups jasmine rice
2 chicken bouillon cubes
¾ pound ground pork
2 cloves garlic, minced
¼ cup light soy sauce
1 teaspoon kosher salt, plus more to taste
½ teaspoon freshly ground black pepper
3-inch piece fresh ginger, peeled and cut into very thin julienne
2 tablespoons chopped fresh cilantro leaves
2 scallions, thinly sliced
Fried Sliced Garlic (recipe follows), to taste

Place the rice in a fine-mesh sieve and rinse under cold water. Drain and transfer to a soup pot. Add 12 cups water and the bouillon cubes. Bring to a boil and cook until the rice is soft and broken down to a porridge, about 45 minutes.

While the porridge is cooking, in a medium bowl, combine the pork, garlic, soy sauce, salt, and pepper.

When the rice is porridge-like, take a pinch of pork between your fingers and drop it into the pot, repeating for all of the pork mixture. Add the ginger and cook until the pork "dumplings" are cooked, about 5 minutes. Taste, and thin with some water if it seems too thick for your tastes. (It should be rich and comforting, but if you want it more soupy, you do you.) Season to taste with more salt. Stir in the cilantro and scallions.

Divide the porridge among bowls and garnish with a sprinkle of fried garlic.

fried sliced garlic

MAKES ¾ CUP

TOTAL TIME: 15 minutes

12 cloves garlic
Canola oil, for frying
Kosher salt

Thinly slice the garlic with a knife or mandoline.

In a large heavy pot, heat 1 inch of oil to 300°F (you'll know it's ready when a garlic slice almost immediately begins to sizzle, but gently, when dropped into the oil).

Add half of the garlic and fry, stirring with a spider or a slotted spoon to help the garlic cook evenly, until it is lightly golden (it will continue to darken as it cools), 2 to 3 minutes. Remove with a spider or a slotted spoon and drain on paper towels. Sprinkle with salt while hot. Repeat with the remaining garlic. (Save the oil after it cools and use it to show your next dish how much you love it.) Fried garlic keeps in an airtight container for up to 2 weeks.

SERVES 4 TO 6

PREP TIME: 15 minutes **TOTAL TIME:** 1 hour 15 minutes

GRILLED GARLIC-SOY SHRIMP

WITH PEPPER'S HOT GREEN PEPPER SAUCE

I have never seen a shrimp in its natural habitat, but I'm convinced they would terrify me more than most anything. That's why I prefer them dead, on my grill, and later, inside my belly.

Mom has two signature sauces that I find myself craving so often that the actual dish is merely a way to consume said sauce. The first is her Red Hot Pepper Sauce (page 107), which we love with meats, and then this bright green hot pepper sauce, which we slather on any and all seafood.

These garlic-soy shrimp are mouthwatering on their own, especially with steamed rice or grilled vegetables, but the seafood sauce takes it to the next level. But be warned! A little goes a long way.

- **1 cup soy sauce**
- **¼ cup finely minced garlic (about 8 cloves)**
- **1 tablespoon freshly ground black pepper**
- **1½ pounds large shrimp (shell-on, head-on if you can stand it)**
- **Pepper's Hot Green Pepper Sauce (recipe follows), for serving**

In a large bowl, combine the soy sauce, garlic, and black pepper. Add the shrimp and toss to coat. Refrigerate for 1 hour.

Preheat a grill, grill pan, or cast-iron skillet over high heat until smoking hot. Remove the shrimp from the marinade, letting it drip off. Place the shrimp on the grill and cook until just opaque and charred on one side, about 2 minutes. Flip and cook 1 minute longer. If cooked shell-on, add an additional 30 seconds cooking time or so and let guests peel and eat. Serve with Pepper's hot green pepper sauce and steamed rice, if desired, or grilled vegetables.

stank dream

Fish sauce, is salty, stinky, and TOTALLY ESSENTIAL. Basically, they pack anchovies and salt into a barrel, then leave it to sit there till the salty fishy juice gets strained out months later. I know how that sounds. I know how it smells. But it makes Thai food—and so many other foods—taste amazing. The smell totally changes when you cook it or mix it with other things. You can buy it at any Asian market, and in most supermarkets on that weird little "International" shelf.

pepper's hot green pepper sauce

MAKES ABOUT ½ CUP

TOTAL TIME: 5 minutes

4 serrano peppers (hot) or 20 green Thai chiles (crazy hot)
6 cloves garlic
3 tablespoons fish sauce
½ tablespoon brown sugar
Juice and zest of ½ lime

In a blender, combine the peppers, garlic, and ¼ cup water and pulse about 15 times to get everything going, then blend until almost smooth (some bits and seeds are OK), about 15 seconds. Transfer to a bowl and stir in the fish sauce, brown sugar, and lime juice. The sauce will keep in the refrigerator for 1 week.

SERVES 4

TOTAL TIME: 20 minutes

POUNDED THAI PAPAYA (OR GREEN BEAN) SALAD

This has ruined me for ALL. OTHER. PAPAYA SALADS. Mom can cook evvvvverything well, but man, she is a papaya salad ninja. Once requested, it's on the table in three minutes and never fails to be perfect. When trying out a new Thai restaurant, I always order two things first: tom yum soup and papaya salad. If their tom yum or papaya salad sucks, the chances of anything else being good are slim to none. It's a rule that's always held true for me.

Made at least five times a week in my household (did you know an Asian Mom lives with us? It's awesome), I live on this before shoots. We add WAY more chile, to the point where my face has a stroke and I can't blink one eye or symmetrically smile, but I finish the entire plate. Serve it with steamed rice and roasted chicken or pork rinds. Seriously. They cut the heat but even if they didn't, they're pork rinds and pork rinds are awesome.

(Oh, and by the way, unless you have a Thai Town lying around, green papaya can be tricky to find, but fear not—this is equally good with green beans or even shredded cucumber.)

- 1 lime, halved
- 1 large jalapeño pepper (pretty hot) or 3 fresh Thai chiles (really hot)
- 1 dried red Thai chile (optional)
- 2 cloves garlic
- 2 tablespoons palm, raw, or light brown sugar
- 10 cherry tomatoes, halved
- 2 tablespoons fish sauce
- 1 pound green papaya or 1 pound green beans
- 3 tablespoons chopped unsalted roasted peanuts (optional)
- Cooked sticky or jasmine rice, for serving

special **EQUIPMENT** Large mortar and pestle (or you can fake it; see recipe)

Cut one-half of the lime into small wedges and place in a large mortar along with the fresh chiles (and dried chile, if using), garlic, and sugar. Crush with the pestle until the chiles are mashed and bruised but not totally pulverized and the sugar is dissolved. Add the tomatoes and pound a few times to bruise the tomatoes. (You can also accomplish this with a plain old bowl and a round-ended cocktail muddler. Or you can chop the garlic first and just mix and mash everything in a mixing bowl. Sorry, Mom.) Squeeze the juice from the remaining lime half (about 1 tablespoon) into the mortar and stir in the fish sauce.

If using green papaya, peel and seed it, then shred with a food processor or mandoline. If using green beans, trim them and cut into 2-inch lengths. You should have about 4 cups of papaya or beans.

Add the papaya or green beans to the mortar and mash and toss lightly. Divide the salad among bowls. If desired, top with the peanuts. Serve with rice.

the thai hotness

Thai bird chiles used to be super hard to find, but now you can buy them at Asian markets and even regular supermarkets. They are hot as hell. If you can't find them, use serrano chiles.

SERVES 8 TO 10

PREP TIME: 20 minutes **TOTAL TIME:** 1 hour

PEPPER'S PORK-STUFFED CUCUMBER SOUP

Half of me, my white half, loves stuffing cheese into things. The other half, my Thai half, loves stuffing meats into things. So 100 percent of me is genetically predisposed to want to stuff things into other things.

John and I love coming home to this soup. It's magic: it has the power to make me fall right to sleep while still feeling light. But if I have it for lunch, I am somehow energized for the day. (???) And if I consistently eat it for a week, I get a flatter stomach (???) from eating pork. (???) It's all very confusing.

Anyhow, more than that, it's just a really f*cking good soup. We love coarsely crushing whole peppercorns in the ol' mortar and pestle, ensuring that every bite of pork has a punch of black pepper, which in turn flavors the cucumber.

Also, I am kind of getting off on the fact you probably haven't had anything like this. Or ever cooked a cucumber until it's tender and spoonable. Trust me. Magic.

- **1 pound ground pork**
- **¼ cup light soy sauce**
- **10 cloves garlic, mashed or finely minced**
- **¼ teaspoon freshly ground black pepper**
- **5 large cucumbers, peeled, ends NOT trimmed**
- **3 chicken bouillon cubes**
- **1 bunch honshimeji mushrooms (see Note), trimmed and separated**
- **¼ cup thinly sliced scallions**

In a bowl, mix together the pork, soy sauce, garlic, and pepper.

Halve the cucumbers crosswise. Using a measuring spoon or a pineapple corer, hollow out the cucumbers so each of them becomes a hollow tube with a solid end. Pack each tube with the pork mixture.

In a large, Dutch oven or wide soup pot, combine 12 cups water and the bouillon cubes and bring to a boil over high heat. Add the stuffed cucumbers, reduce the heat, and simmer for 30 minutes. (YES, YOU ARE COOKING CUCUMBERS. THEY ARE DELICIOUS.) Add the mushrooms and cook until the pork is cooked through and the cucumber is tender, about 15 minutes longer.

Transfer the cucumbers, mushrooms, and some of the broth to bowls, then serve with the scallions on top.

note // Honshimeji mushrooms are like cuter, smaller, more tender shiitakes. Find them in Asian markets and other places exotic mushrooms are sold.

SERVES 3 TO 4

PREP TIME: 15 minutes **TOTAL TIME:** 25 minutes

PAD GRAPOW CHICKEN
(BASIL CHICKEN)

- **1¼ pounds boneless, skinless chicken breasts, sliced into thin strips**
- **2 tablespoons oyster sauce**
- **2 tablespoons light soy sauce**
- **5 cloves garlic**
- **1 serrano chile (or as many fresh Thai chiles as you can stand)**
- **2 tablespoons vegetable oil**
- **3 cups fresh Thai or regular basil leaves**
- **Cooked jasmine rice, for serving**

Us Thais lovvvvvvvve us some *pad grapow*—stir-fried basil. This dish can be made with chicken, beef, seafood, or vegetables—the only must is the sweet spice of basil—preferably, of course, Thai basil.

One of the first things I learned on my excursion to Thailand for the Oriental Hotel's cooking school (they let anyone in—literally a baby went), this recipe is so widely loved I couldn't not have it in the book.

How wide, you ask? (1) That's what she said, (2) wide enough that it is my white papa Ron's absolute favorite. Throw a crispy fried egg on top and your last name will end in porn in no time. THAT'S A THAI JOKE, U WOULDN'T UNDERSTANDSOPORN.

In a bowl, toss the chicken with the oyster sauce and soy sauce and marinate for 10 minutes. Mash the garlic and chile in a mortar and pestle until finely smashed (or mince with a knife).

In a large skillet or wok, heat the oil over medium-high heat. When the oil is shimmering-hot, add the garlic-chile mixture and cook until fragrant, about 30 seconds. Increase the heat to high, add the chicken, and cook, stirring, until just cooked through, about 4 minutes. Add the basil and cook until wilted, about 1 minute.

Serve with the rice.

PARTY TIME

Opposite: Stretchy Artichoke, Spinach, and Buffalo Chicken Dip (PAGE 144)

SERVES 4 TO 6 AS AN APPETIZER

PREP TIME: 45 minutes **TOTAL TIME:** 3 hours

CHICKEN SATAY
WITH PEANUT SAUCE

In restaurants, I find chicken satay to be a bit dry and lame, but I order it for the sole purpose of cramming peanut sauce into my belly. But oh, I had a dream. A dream to create a delicious, Thai-inspired coconut-grilled chicken, juicy little meat suckers to complement the spicy peanut sauce. Achievement: Unlocked.

for the **CHICKEN AND MARINADE**

- 1 (14-ounce) can full-fat coconut milk (NOT light)
- 8 cloves garlic, minced
- ¼ cup chopped fresh cilantro leaves
- 2 tablespoons light brown sugar
- 4 teaspoons kosher salt
- 1 tablespoon ground turmeric
- 1 tablespoon finely grated fresh ginger
- 1 teaspoon ground cumin
- 1 pound chicken tenders (about 12)

for the **SATAY SAUCE**

- ½ cup creamy peanut butter, preferably not natural-style
- ¼ cup (packed) light brown sugar
- 5 cloves garlic, minced
- 1 teaspoon finely grated fresh ginger
- 3 tablespoons light soy sauce
- 1½ tablespoons Sriracha
- 1 tablespoon rice vinegar

for the **SWEET HOT PEPPER SAUCE**

- ½ cup sugar
- 1 tablespoon distilled white vinegar
- ½ seedless cucumber, chopped
- 1 shallot, finely chopped
- 1 jalapeño pepper or fresh Thai chile, minced
- Kosher salt

special **EQUIPMENT**

- 8 wooden skewers, soaked in water for 30 minutes

MARINATE THE CHICKEN: In a bowl, combine the coconut milk, garlic, cilantro, brown sugar, salt, turmeric, ginger, and cumin in a bowl. Add the chicken tenders, cover, and marinate for at least 2 hours and up to 12 hours in the refrigerator.

MAKE THE SATAY SAUCE: In a bowl, combine the peanut butter, brown sugar, garlic, ginger, soy sauce, Sriracha, vinegar, and ¼ cup water, thinning with additional water if you prefer a thinner sauce.

MAKE THE SWEET HOT PEPPER SAUCE: In a bowl, combine the sugar, ½ cup water, the vinegar, cucumber, shallot, and chile. Season to taste with salt.

COOK THE CHICKEN: Heat a grill or grill pan over medium-high heat until hot. Remove the chicken tenders from their marinade, letting the excess drop back into the bowl. Thread each chicken tender on a skewer and grill until cooked through but still juicy, 2 to 3 minutes per side.

Serve the chicken with the satay sauce and sweet hot pepper sauce.

MAKES 12 PIECES / SERVES 4 TO 6

PREP TIME: 10 minutes **TOTAL TIME:** 15 minutes

STEAK BITES
WITH MELTY BLUE CHEESE BUTTER

- 2 ounces soft, creamy-style blue cheese, at room temperature
- 1 tablespoon butter, slightly softened
- ½ pound New York strip steak (see Note), trimmed of excess fat
- ½ teaspoon kosher salt
- 3 tablespoons roughly cracked black pepper
- 2 tablespoons canola oil
- ½ cup crushed potato sticks (the kind you get at 7-Eleven or the corner store, nothing fancy!)

Aaaah, my single-bite delights. Pepper-crusted steak with oozy blue cheese butter seems classy, so sex it up with some crushed-up potato sticks. Trying to impress a date? Maybe add a tiny little roasted potato on there. Maybe add a cherry tomato if they have a huge mouth. But if you go down that path, you better keep that classy sh*t up the entire relationship. That's why I like to start with the potato sticks. Lets the dude know exactly what he's getting.

In a small bowl, mash the blue cheese and butter with a fork until smooth.

Pat the meat dry with paper towels and cut into twelve 1-inch cubes. Season it all over with the salt. Place the cracked pepper in a shallow dish and press the steak cubes into the pepper on all sides to form a pepper crust.

In a medium cast-iron or heavy skillet, heat the oil over medium-high heat. When shimmering-hot, add the steak cubes and cook on all sides until medium-rare, about 30 seconds per side. Remove the steak from the skillet by stabbing each cube with a wooden, metal, or bamboo skewer. Squash about 1 teaspoon of the blue cheese butter on top of the meat (it will begin to melt down the sides if you play your cards right), then press a few potato sticks into the cheese.

note

Try to get as rectangular and evenly thick (about 1 inch) piece of steak as you can. You can buy it a little bigger and trim it down to get a perfect half-pound rectangle.

MAKES 8 ROLLS / SERVES 4 TO 8

PREP TIME: 20 minutes **TOTAL TIME:** 40 minutes

SHRIMP SUMMER ROLLS

- **4 to 6 red leaf lettuce leaves**
- **Kosher salt**
- **8 medium shrimp, peeled**
- **1 ounce thin Asian rice noodles (vermicelli)**
- **8 large or 16 small basil leaves**
- **1 medium carrot, cut into 3-inch-long thin julienne strips**
- **1 avocado, thinly sliced**
- **8 large or 16 medium mint leaves**
- **8 (8-inch) round rice paper wrappers (you can find these in Asian markets)**
- **Thai sweet chili sauce and hoisin sauce, for serving**

Spring rolls are my sh*t. Summer rolls, I can't lie . . . it took me a bit to warm up to them. I mean they aren't even fried? What is that about? But there is something so deliciously light and beautiful about them, and the rice paper wrappers get so good and chewy. I mean I barely even think about rolling pork belly into them.

Also, I have no idea why, but I have really punctual friends. So to punish them, I throw them onto my summer roll assembly line when it's party time. You would (not) be surprised by how excited people are to roll when paid with cheap tequila.

Rinse the lettuce and pat dry. Remove and discard the center ribs and cut the leaves into 3 × 1-inch rectangles. You want to end up with 16 pieces.

Fill a 4-quart saucepan halfway with water, generously salt the water, and bring to a boil over high heat. Add the shrimp and cook until just done, about 2 minutes. Remove the pan from the heat. Remove the shrimp with a slotted spoon, rinse with cold water, and dry on paper towels. Cut off the tails and halve them lengthwise.

Place the rice noodles in the saucepan of still-hot water to soften, about 10 minutes. Drain in a colander and rinse with cold water until cool.

Clear a large work area and line up bowls with the lettuce, shrimp, rice noodles, basil, carrot, avocado, and mint. Fill a clean skillet with warm water for soaking the rice paper wrappers (have more warm water for replenishing to maintain temperature as necessary).

Arrange a damp clean towel on a work surface. Working one at a time, slide a rice paper wrapper into the skillet of warm water to moisten for a few seconds, until it begins to soften but is not completely translucent. Remove from the water and place on the damp towel (the wrappers will continue to soften until they're a little sticky and chewy).

To start rolling, place 1 large or 2 small basil leaves on the center line, about 2½ inches from the edge of the wrapper. Arrange 2 lettuce pieces on top, then top with about 2 tablespoons rice noodles, some carrots, an avocado slice, and 2 shrimp halves. Top with 1 large or 2 medium mint leaves. Gently pull the bottom of the wrapper over the filling, then fold in the sides as though you were making a burrito. Roll up tight and place on a plate lined with a damp paper towel. Cover with another damp paper towel and repeat with the remaining wrappers and ingredients.

Serve immediately with Thai sweet chili sauce and hoisin sauce.

paper made of rice, so nice

You can buy rice paper wrappers in Asian markets, where in Vietnamese they're called *bánh tráng*. These dry, translucent sheets start out looking like giant circles of fresh pasta, but then they're dried on bamboo mats, which creates their cool ridged pattern. A quick dip in warm or lukewarm water will turn them into amazingly chewy skins. (Sadly their cool pattern goes away when they go for their short swim.)

MAKES 16 POPPERS

PREP TIME: 25 minutes **TOTAL TIME:** 45 minutes

HAWAIIAN PIZZA JALAPEÑO POPPERS

I haaaaaaate that bacon has become so mainstream cool. Bacon ice cream, bacon soda, bacon TOOTHPASTE. Bacon has now become some sort of clickbait fodder, and I will no longer have you degrade the sanctity and beauty of bacon!!!!

Therefore, I am sorry, but I cannot give you bacon-wrapped jalapeño poppers. You can find that sh*t online. We're here to surprise and excite people, so ladies and gentlemen, please welcome: the Hawaiian pizza jalapeño popper.

Perhaps I am in the minority here, but I LOVE HAWAIIAN PIZZA. But there is always that one person that is just dead-set on talking about how much they hate it. They're insane, and they're wrong, and now I put it in a popper and this book is gonna sell and guess what? I'm gonna buy more Hawaiian pizzas with the cash just to piss you off. (See photograph, page 133.)

- 8 medium jalapeño peppers
- 20 pieces very thinly sliced deli ham (about ½ pound)
- 4 ounces cream cheese, at room temperature
- ¾ cup shredded mozzarella cheese
- 2 scallions (green parts only), sliced
- ¼ cup chopped cooked bacon (4 slices)
- ¼ cup chopped fresh pineapple plus 8 (1-inch) cubes pineapple
- 1 large garlic clove, minced
- ¼ teaspoon kosher salt
- ¼ teaspoon freshly ground black pepper
- 8 cherry or grape tomatoes

special **EQUIPMENT**

- 16 long wooden toothpicks, soaked in hot water for 10 minutes

Preheat the oven to 425°F. Line a baking sheet with foil.

Halve the jalapeños lengthwise and discard the seeds and ribs.

Finely chop 4 slices of the ham and place them in a medium bowl. Add the cream cheese, mozzarella, scallion greens, bacon, chopped pineapple, garlic, salt, and black pepper and combine.

Fill each jalapeño half with a heaping tablespoon of the filling. Fold each ham slice in half and wrap each filled jalapeño half with the ham. Skewer a toothpick with a pineapple cube or tomato (so you'll have 8 of each), then skewer it through the wrapped jalapeños.

Arrange the poppers on the lined baking sheet and bake until the cheese is bubbling and the jalapeños are softened, about 20 minutes. Serve hot.

peeling and coring a pineapple

Cut off the top and bottom of the pineapple and stand it up on its end. Using a sharp knife, cut the peel away, cutting just as much as you need to get all those little spines while following the shape of the pineapple. Quarter the pineapple lengthwise. This will expose the woody core, which you can just cut off by cutting down the length of the quarter.

MAKES 8 CUPS / SERVES 8 TO 12

PREP TIME: 15 minutes **TOTAL TIME:** 1 hour

I CAN'T BELIEVE IT'S NOT GARDETTO'S

- **2 bagels (preferably pumpernickel), sliced into small, thin rounds (3½ cups)**
- **3 cups Chex cereal (rice, wheat, or corn variety)**
- **1 cup broken grissini breadsticks**
- **1 cup broken pretzel sticks**
- **1 stick (4 ounces) unsalted butter**
- **6 cloves garlic, roughly chopped**
- **1 small onion, cut into 1-inch wedges**
- **¼ cup Worcestershire sauce**
- **1 tablespoon Cholula or other hot sauce**
- **¼ teaspoon freshly ground black pepper**

Screw the destination. Road trips and plane rides are made for stocking up on gossip rags and junk food raiding, a.k.a. Gardetto's time. I also owe all my genius to the deliciousness that is Gardetto's snack mix. It's the only reason I stayed alert in middle school (where you become a genius). I used to separate each little component and suck the flavor off them individually and then put it back into the bag to throw away (story of my life), all while learning about how horrible a man Christopher Columbus was. Anyhoo, the OG Gardetto's is filled with random words they didn't teach me in middle school, so this crunchy, spicy, salty, tangy recipe is a breath of fresh, homemade air. (See photograph, overleaf.)

Preheat the oven to 350°F.

Arrange the bagel rounds on a large rimmed baking sheet in one layer and bake until crisp, 10 to 12 minutes. Transfer them to a large bowl and add the cereal, breadsticks, and pretzel sticks. Leave the oven on.

Meanwhile, in a small saucepan, combine the butter, garlic, and onion and bring to a simmer over medium heat. Cook until the garlic is just turning brown at the edges, about 15 minutes. Remove from the heat and strain the butter into a bowl (discard the solids). Whisk in the Worcestershire, Cholula, and black pepper.

Add the butter mixture to the dry mix, toss to evenly coat, pour onto the baking sheet, and spread it out into one layer. Bake until crisp, about 25 minutes, stirring once midway through baking. Cool and store in an airtight container for up to 1 week.

// I Can't Believe It's Not Gardetto's (PAGE 129)

United States of America
DELTA
BOARD TIME
4:09P
DEPARTS: 4:59 PM
ARRIVES: 8:08 PM
SEAT
3F
WINDOW
FIRST
E2830H
UA 1199 3F
BSEE34
Crossw
Across
1 Sajak of Wheel of Fortune
4 The Simpsons grandpa
7 E-_ (tobacco alt.)
10 Jelly container
13 Rapper-actor _-T
14 Payment to the IRS
15 Saturday Night Live alum Gasteyer
16 Bagel center
17 TV political drama series with Rob Lowe
20 Habit-kicking clinic
21 _-Pro (Will Ferrell movie)
22 Jeremy of Reversal of Fortune
23 Laura of I Am Sam
24 More pleasant
26 Of help
29 Matt of The Bourne Identity
32 Citi Field ballplayer
34 _ Sharkey (Don Rickles show)
35 _ lime pie
36 One _ time (singly)
37 Get on in years
39 "Confessions" singer
41 Hand-_ coordination
42 Two-piece swimwear
44 Rest _ (roadside stop)
45 Sunbather's shade
47 Flower stalk
48 2014 Rob movie
51 "What's _ for me?"
73 Get out of bed
75 "Long _, no see!"
76 Mixes with a spoon
78 Pinocchio's protuberance
82 Popeye's gal, _ Oyl
84 1992 movie with Rob
86 Chips brand with owl logo
87 Make a boo-boo
88 Golden Girl McClanahan
89 Gear tooth
90 Pecan or pistachio
91 Sheep's call
92 Extra-wide, on a shoe box
93 Go _ (lose it)
Down
1 Olive throwaways
2 Feel sore
3 Rain cats and dogs
4 Had a bite
5 No-frills

MAKES 12

PREP TIME: 20 minutes **TOTAL TIME:** 35 minutes

SECRETLY SPICY DEVILED EGGS

6 eggs
Kosher salt
2 pieces bacon, cooked crisp and finely chopped
¼ cup mayonnaise
1 teaspoon yellow mustard
1 tablespoon sweet pickle relish
Freshly ground black pepper
Sriracha (in its squeeze bottle)
12 thin slices pickled jalapeño peppers and/or gherkins

Criteria to be my friend: You must never call and you must love deviled eggs.* Parties and holidays were created for deviled eggs. There is just something so . . . cozy about them to me. When I see them, I am reminded of all the times I made them for people I love. These are usually the first thing I make for occasions. While "deviled eggs" may not be the sexiest thing to say aloud (the name screams "Grandma"), they never last long. Plus, mine have a creepy secret flavor basement of Sriracha. That is so not Grandma.

* *You may call if you want to talk about deviled eggs.*

Fill a bowl halfway with ice and water. In a saucepan, combine the eggs with cold water to cover by 1 inch. Add 1 tablespoon salt and bring to a boil over high heat. Remove the pan from the heat, cover, and let sit for 9 minutes. Transfer the eggs to the bowl of ice water and let sit for 5 minutes.

Peel the eggs under cold running water. Halve the eggs lengthwise, then trim a tiny slice off the wobbly underside of each egg half, so the eggs will sit flat. Carefully pry out the yolks and transfer to a bowl.

Add the bacon, mayo, mustard, relish, and salt and pepper to taste to the yolks and mash until smooth. Squirt a dab of Sriracha inside the empty egg whites. (Here's your hot sauce surprise!) Fill a sandwich-size plastic bag with the yolk filling (if you fold the edges of the bag down, turning about half the bag inside out, the bag will be easier to fill). Force all of the filling to one corner of the bag, snip off the end with scissors, and pipe the filling into the egg whites. Garnish with the sliced jalapeños or gherkins—or both.

Secretly Spicy Deviled Eggs with Crab, Cream Cheese, and Scallion Wontons (PAGE 134); Hawaiian Pizza Jalapeño Poppers (PAGE 128)

MAKES 36 WONTONS / SERVES 6 TO 8

PREP TIME: 25 minutes **TOTAL TIME:** 35 minutes

CRAB, CREAM CHEESE, AND SCALLION WONTONS

My favorite guilty-pleasure restaurants, ranked:

5. Outback Steakhouse (Bloomin' Onion)
4. Applebee's (Riblets)
3. Islands (Teriyaki pineapple chicken tacos)
2. Red Robin (Ranch dressing)
1. P.F.-uckin-Chang's (Crab wontons)

This dish (and P.F. Chang's in general) is about as Chinese as McDonald's is Scottish, but at least you can make these in the comfort of your own home without staring at a statue of a Mongolian warrior with a single tear coming from his eye. Anyway, I have NO shame in my P.F. Chang's wonton-loving game. Home-fried wontons are a freaking delight. Fun to stuff, quick to cook, piping hot when they're finally popped into your mouth.

for the **DIPPING SAUCE**

- 3 tablespoons Chinese hot mustard
- 1½ tablespoons honey
- 1 teaspoon soy sauce

for the **WONTONS**

- 4 ounces lump crabmeat, picked over to remove shells
- 4 ounces cream cheese, at room temperature
- ½ teaspoon kosher salt
- ¼ teaspoon freshly ground black pepper
- 1 teaspoon Sriracha
- 1 teaspoon Chinese hot mustard
- 3 tablespoons sliced scallions (about 2 scallions)
- 36 (4-inch) square wonton skins
- 1 egg, beaten
- Vegetable oil, for frying

MAKE THE DIPPING SAUCE: In a small bowl, combine the mustard, honey, and soy sauce.

MAKE THE WONTONS: In a food processor, combine the crabmeat, cream cheese, salt, black pepper, Sriracha, and hot mustard until smooth. Fold in the scallions.

Working with 4 or 5 wontons at a time, arrange the wonton skins with a point facing you (like a diamond). Spoon 1 teaspoon of the filling onto the skin, then brush all of the edges of the wonton skin with egg. Fold the top point down and over the filling to meet the bottom point and press down, squeezing the air out of the wonton and sealing the wonton into a triangle shape. Dab one of the points on the long side with a little more egg, then pull it toward the opposite point and pinch the two together to form a dumpling. Repeat with the remaining wonton skins and filling.

In a medium saucepan that is at least 6 inches deep, heat 4 inches of oil over medium-high heat until it reaches 350°F on a deep-fry thermometer. (If you don't have a thermometer, a small piece of wonton wrapper should sizzle immediately, but not burn, when dropped into the hot oil.)

Using a slotted spoon, carefully lower a few wontons at a time into the hot oil, leaving enough room for them to float around in the oil. Fry until the skins puff and brown, about 2 minutes, then remove them with the slotted spoon and drain on paper towels. Fry the rest, and serve with the honey-mustard sauce for dipping.

MAKES 8 SLIDERS / SERVES 4 TO 8

PREP TIME: 15 minutes **TOTAL TIME:** 20 minutes

KING'S HAWAIIAN BLPTS

- 2 slices cored fresh pineapple
- 8 King's Hawaiian slider rolls, split
- Unsalted butter, softened (I like a lot)
- Mayo (as much as you like)
- 4 lettuce leaves, cut to fit the sandwiches
- 1 large vine-ripened tomato, cut into 8 slices
- 8 slices bacon, cooked (see Note) and halved crosswise
- 1 sweet onion, thinly sliced into rings

Hawaii comes through with so many wonderful gifts that I almost feel like they're just trying to make up for poi and Adam Sandler movies. King's Hawaiian sweet bread, golden pineapples, chocolate-covered macadamia nuts, giant roto pigs, Spam musubi (don't start!! I love Spam).

The BLT has been done more ways than Beyoncé's hair, but the grilled pineapple turns this one into sweet caramelized, bacony, mayo-y, smushy roll heaven. Even Arby's can't copy that. (OK, no shade, but, Arby's, I posted my BLT on King's Hawaiian rolls, then you favorited my tweet, then you came out with a King's Hawaiian BLT sandwich a couple months later. I am too busy to let this case get caught up in the U.S. criminal justice system, so you can just send me some roast beef and we will call it even.)

Position a rack 4 to 6 inches from the heating element and preheat the broiler.

Arrange the pineapple slices on a baking sheet and broil until browned on both sides. Let cool slightly, then quarter them. (You can also grill the pineapple on a hot grill or grill pan over medium-high heat.) Leave the broiler on.

Spread the rolls with butter and arrange on another baking sheet. Broil them until deeply golden, 1 to 2 minutes.

Spread mayo on the rolls, then layer the lettuce, tomato, bacon, onions, and a pineapple wedge on the roll bottoms. Top with the other half of the rolls.

note

See Garlic-Roasted Bacon (page 17) for my favorite way to cook bacon. Follow that method, just without the garlic.

SERVES 6

PREP TIME: 15 minutes **TOTAL TIME:** 30 minutes

CHICKEN LETTUCE WRAPS

for the **SAUCE**

- 3 tablespoons Thai sweet chili sauce
- 3 tablespoons hoisin sauce
- 3 tablespoons light soy sauce
- 2 tablespoons Sriracha
- 2 tablespoons vegetable oil
- 1 teaspoon sesame oil
- 1½ tablespoons unseasoned rice vinegar
- 2 tablespoons minced garlic (about 4 cloves)
- 1 tablespoon minced fresh ginger

for the **FILLING**

- 1 pound ground chicken
- 3 tablespoons vegetable oil
- 8 scallions, thinly sliced, whites and greens kept separate
- 1 tablespoon minced garlic (about 2 cloves)
- 1 tablespoon minced fresh ginger
- ½ pound white mushrooms, trimmed, cleaned, and finely chopped
- ½ cup finely diced canned water chestnuts
- 1 small red bell pepper, finely chopped

- 2 heads butter lettuce, leaves separated

I am one lettuce-wrapping son of a gun. Ninety percent of my brain capacity is filled with Rain Man–esque food equations on how I can make something low-carb, or as I prefer to call it, lower-carb. Using seaweed sheets, portobello mushroom "buns," and thinly sliced zucchini actually do the job quite nicely, but lettuce-wrapping is of course the easiest way.

Every single time I make this dish, I find myself burying my head in the fridge all night, scooping and scraping for every chicken bit possible with my bare hands. Filling and healthy and freaking yummy. No bacon. No cheese. No starch. I am almost embarrassed to say I love it.

MAKE THE SAUCE: In a bowl, combine the chili sauce, hoisin, soy sauce, Sriracha, vegetable oil, sesame oil, vinegar, garlic, and ginger.

MAKE THE FILLING: In a bowl, mix 2 tablespoons of the sauce into the ground chicken.

In a large skillet, heat 2 tablespoons of the vegetable oil over medium-high heat. When shimmering-hot, add the chicken and cook, breaking up the meat with a wooden spoon, until browned, 5 to 6 minutes. Transfer the meat to a plate and set aside.

Add the remaining 1 tablespoon oil to the skillet, then add the scallion whites, garlic, and ginger and cook, stirring, for 1 minute. Add the mushrooms and cook, stirring, until they release their liquid, 3 to 4 minutes. Return the chicken to the pan, then add the water chestnuts, bell pepper, and the rest of the sauce and cook, stirring, until cooked through and the liquid has reduced and thickened slightly, 3 to 4 minutes. Stir in the scallion greens.

Transfer the mixture to a bowl and set out with the lettuce leaves.

gimme that hotness, sugar

Sweet chili sauce is a staple in Thai food, usually served with charcoal-grilled chicken. YASSS. It's basically light syrup cooked down with red chiles and we love this stuff to dip our summer rolls into. As an ingredient, it adds sweetness and spice to dishes, and it's great on a sandwich. These days you can find it in the Asian people part of a regular ol' supermarket.

SERVES 8 TO 10

PREP TIME: 15 minutes **TOTAL TIME:** 4 hours 45 minutes

JOHN'S FRIED CHICKEN WINGS WITH SPICY HONEY BUTTER

In the sea of things John does right, his fried chicken is the . . . I dunno . . . whatever the king of the sea is. I guess that *Little Mermaid* guy with the giant fork.

There is nothing in this world I crave more than this eerily simple party staple of ours. Harvesting the crumbs from post-party plates tops the list of things I am not exactly proud of.

I prefer it as little wings and drumettes as I've calculated the skin to meat ratio and determined I get more crispy skin by gnawing on the little guys. And then we decided to start drizzling it with Cholula honey butter.

We have problems.

for the **CHICKEN AND BRINE**

- 6 tablespoons Lawry's Seasoning Salt
- 2½ tablespoons garlic powder
- 2 tablespoons cayenne pepper
- 5 pounds chicken wings and drumettes

for the **BREADING AND FRYING**

- Canola oil, for deep-frying
- 4 cups all-purpose flour
- 2 tablespoons Lawry's Seasoning Salt
- 1 tablespoon cayenne pepper

for the **SPICY HONEY BUTTER**

- 1 stick (4 ounces) unsalted butter, melted and cooled
- 4 tablespoons Cholula hot sauce (sorry, it has to be Cholula)
- 2 tablespoons honey
- ¾ teaspoon kosher salt, plus more to taste

special **EQUIPMENT**

- Deep-fry or candy thermometer

BRINE THE CHICKEN: In a really big pot or a 2-gallon zip-top plastic bag, combine 10 cups cold water, the seasoning salt, garlic powder, and cayenne. Add the chicken, cover, and refrigerate for at least 4 hours and up to 24.

BREAD AND FRY THE CHICKEN: Fill a soup pot with 6 inches of oil, making sure there are at least 4 inches of clearance between the oil and the lip of the pot. Heat the oil over medium heat until it reaches 365°F on a deep-fry thermometer, or prepare a deep fryer according to the manufacturer's instructions.

In a big bowl, combine the flour, seasoning salt, and cayenne. A few at a time, remove the wings from the brine and toss them in the flour mixture until coated really well, then place on a baking sheet while you coat the rest.

When the oil is ready, turn the heat up to medium-high and carefully slip in the wings, adding just enough so that there's still plenty of space around each wing. (If it feels safer, use tongs to add the wings; whatever you do, don't just drop them in! Splashing hot oil is bad.) Fry the wings until golden and crispy, about 13 minutes per batch. Drain the wings on plenty of paper towels. Fry the remaining chicken, letting the oil come back to temperature between batches.

MAKE THE SPICY HONEY BUTTER: While the chicken is frying, in a bowl, whisk together the melted butter, Cholula, honey, and salt until incorporated. Taste and add more salt if necessary.

Slather the wings with the spicy honey butter and eat that chaacken!

SERVES 6 TO 8

PREP TIME: 20 minutes **TOTAL TIME:** 3 hours 30 minutes

STRETCHY ARTICHOKE, SPINACH, AND BUFFALO CHICKEN DIP

for the **CHICKEN**

- ½ cup Cholula hot sauce
- 1 stick (4 ounces) butter, melted and slightly cooled
- 1 teaspoon kosher salt
- ¼ teaspoon freshly ground black pepper
- 2 boneless, skinless chicken breasts

Your cheese-filled mouth will struggle to muster small talk when you have this at your next function. I have never had a single leftover with this bad boy. It goes quicker than anything I ever make, which sucks because I barely have time to tell people how I made the pita chips myself (no one ever cares). From the Cholula-marinated chicken to the salty artichokes to the hot, bubbling cheese—every single bite is the heaven we hope exists.

MARINATE AND COOK THE CHICKEN: In a medium bowl, combine the hot sauce, melted butter, salt, and pepper. Add the chicken, toss to coat, cover, and marinate for 2 hours at room temp or up to 8 hours, refrigerated.

Preheat the oven to 350°F.

Remove the chicken from the marinade, place on a baking sheet, and bake until just cooked through, 14 to 15 minutes. When cool enough to handle, shred with your hands or 2 forks into bite-size chunks. Leave the oven on for the dip.

// *recipe continues*

for the **DIP**

- 2 (10-ounce) packages frozen chopped spinach, thawed and squeezed dry (see Note)
- 2 (14.5-ounce) cans water-packed artichoke hearts, drained, squeezed dry (see Note), and chopped
- 1 cup mayonnaise
- 2 cups shredded mozzarella cheese
- ¾ cup finely grated Parmigiano-Reggiano cheese
- 3 cloves garlic, minced
- 1 tablespoon finely chopped fresh oregano or 1½ teaspoons dried
- 1 teaspoon kosher salt
- ¼ teaspoon freshly ground black pepper
- ½ cup blue cheese crumbles

Spiced Pita Chips (recipe follows), for serving

MAKE THE DIP: Coat an oval ceramic 2-quart baking dish with cooking spray or butter.

In a large bowl, mix together the spinach, artichokes, mayo, mozzarella, Parm, garlic, oregano, salt, and pepper. Stir in the shredded chicken. Spread the dip into the baking dish and dot with the blue cheese.

Bake until golden and bubbling, 35 to 40 minutes. Serve with the pita chips.

note

To really get the extra liquid out of the spinach and artichokes, pile them in the center of a big clean kitchen towel and roll up the towel. Twist the ends toward each other and keep twisting until you've wrung out as much liquid as humanly possible!

spiced pita chips

MAKES 32 CHIPS / SERVES 6 TO 8

PREP TIME: 5 minutes **TOTAL TIME:** 20 minutes

- 3 tablespoons butter, melted
- 2 tablespoons olive oil
- ½ teaspoon cayenne pepper
- ½ teaspoon ground cumin
- ½ teaspoon paprika
- ½ teaspoon garlic powder
- ½ teaspoon kosher salt
- ¼ teaspoon freshly ground black pepper
- 4 pitas, cut into 8 wedges each

Preheat the oven to 350°F.

In a large bowl, combine the melted butter, olive oil, cayenne, cumin, paprika, garlic powder, salt, and black pepper. Add the pita wedges and toss gently to coat. Spread in a single layer on 2 baking sheets and bake, tossing once, until the wedges are browned and crisp at the edges, but still very slightly soft in the center (the chips will harden as they cool), 10 to 15 minutes (depending on thickness of pita). Note: If you like a crunchier chip, bake for a few more minutes, until there is no softness in the center.

Cool completely before serving.

SERVES 6

PREP TIME: 10 minutes **TOTAL TIME:** 1 hour 10 minutes

CHEESY GUACAMOLE

- **3 large Hass avocados**
- **3 tablespoons fresh lime juice**
- **½ teaspoon cayenne pepper**
- **½ teaspoon ground cumin**
- **½ teaspoon kosher salt**
- **1 cup coarsely grated sharp cheddar cheese**
- **½ medium onion, diced**
- **2 Roma (plum) tomatoes, seeded and diced**
- **½ jalapeño pepper, seeded and finely minced**
- **2 cloves garlic, minced**
- **¼ cup chopped fresh cilantro leaves**

CHEESE IN GUACAMOLE. Yes. Cheesy sharp cheddar bombs in every bite, and probably the most controversial recipe I have ever created. Guacamole is a *sacred* thing to people. Adding cheese to it is kind of like when Bravo introduces a new Housewife. You want to hate her. You don't like change. But she grows on you and, eventually, you can't watch the show any other way.

I have to give credit where credit is due. My ex-boyfriend's dad first introduced me to this treat. And I can tell that John so badly wants to hate it, but he can't. It's too good.

Halve the avocadoes and scoop the flesh into a large bowl. Add 1½ tablespoons of the lime juice, the cayenne, cumin, and salt and mash with a potato masher until chunky. Fold in the cheddar, onion, tomatoes, jalapeño, garlic, cilantro, and remaining 1½ tablespoons lime juice. Press plastic wrap into the surface of the guacamole (this prevents it from turning brown) and let sit at room temperature for 1 hour before serving to let the flavors meld.

SERVES 6

PREP TIME: 10 minutes **TOTAL TIME:** 50 minutes

FRITO PIE BAR

- 6 (1-ounce) bags Fritos corn chips
- John's Chili (recipe follows; see Note)
- Cheesy Guacamole (page 147)
- 1 cup sour cream
- 1 cup shredded cheddar or pepper jack cheese
- ½ cup sliced pickled jalapeño peppers
- 4 scallions, chopped

There is not one aspect of this game-day dish than can possibly go wrong. John's chili, poured into individual bags of Fritos, surrounded by bowls upon bowls of self-serve toppings. Not to mention it also makes for Instagram-like heaven. But please don't turn your Sunday football party into a hashtag. Hashtags are ridiculous. More than three is cringeworthy. More than six makes me happy we found a new planet that can sustain human life. Anyhow, make this and lay it out for people to serve themselves. It's #good and I'm #hungry.

Using scissors, carefully cut open the Fritos bags to create pouches. Ladle chili over the chips, then top with guacamole, and any or all condiments in the amounts you like.

john's chili

SERVES 6 TO 8

- 1 pound ground beef
- 1 medium onion, chopped
- 1 cup chopped mushrooms
- 2 tablespoons seasoning salt, such as Lawry's
- 3 tablespoons chili powder
- 1 teaspoon cayenne pepper
- 2 tablespoons minced garlic (about 3 cloves)
- 2 (15-ounce) cans tomato sauce
- 2 (15-ounce) cans kidney beans, drained
- 2 tablespoons light brown sugar

Heat a large pot over medium heat. When hot, add the ground beef, onion, mushrooms, seasoning salt, chili powder, and cayenne. Cook, breaking up the meat with a wooden spoon, until the mushrooms release their liquid and the meat is no longer pink, 7 to 8 minutes. Stir in the garlic and cook for 1 additional minute. Add 2 cups water, the tomato sauce, kidney beans, and brown sugar and bring to a boil. Reduce the heat to medium-low and simmer until the chili thickens and the liquid reduces slightly, 35 to 40 minutes. The chili tastes better the longer you let the flavors mingle.

note // The recipe for John's Chili makes a lot, so whatever doesn't get used in the Fritos bags, save to eat as a meal.

Fritos
The ORIGINAL
CORN CHIPS

tos

SERVES 6 TO 8

PREP TIME: 10 minutes **TOTAL TIME:** 30 minutes

ROASTED JALAPEÑO AND CHORIZO QUESO

So apparently there's a thing called Ambien eating, where you get up at 4 a.m. and eat ten sleeves of saltines and don't remember until you wake up the next morning in a bed full of crumbs and waxed paper bags. But I think there also must be Ambien cooking because I don't really remember *making* this sick and delicious queso—I basically snapped back to attention to find John, half asleep on the couch with the bowl scraped clean next to him. Wait! It's coming back to me now! We were just hanging out one night and the options were (a) Jack in the Box delivery or (b) Nobu L.A. (I know, we're a little food schizo). Then I realized all I wanted was a bag of chips and a dip that ate like a dinner, so I got some chorizo, fried it up with onions, and added roasted jalapeños and fresh tomatoes, because nothing's better than a can of Ro-Tel, but I didn't have any in the house and I'm crafty like that. This queso—with Velveeta, of course—will ruin you for any other.

- **6 large jalapeño peppers**
- **1 tablespoon vegetable oil**
- **½ pound fresh Mexican chorizo, casings removed**
- **¾ cup diced onion**
- **¾ cup diced tomato**
- **1 pound Velveeta cheese, cubed**

Preheat the oven to 500°F.

Halve and seed 5 of the jalapeños, toss with the vegetable oil in a bowl, and arrange on a small baking sheet, skin-side up. Roast until very dark, about 15 minutes. Cool and finely chop. Finely mince the remaining raw jalapeño, seeds and all. (Don't touch your eyes, peen, or vag. Seriously.)

In a heavy skillet, cook the chorizo and onion over medium-high heat, breaking up the meat with a wooden spoon, until the onions soften and the meat browns, 7 to 9 minutes. Stir in the tomato and roasted jalapeños, then add the Velveeta. Reduce the heat to medium-low, cover, and heat until melty, 2 to 3 minutes. Add the raw jalapeño and stir until the mixture is smooth.

Stir and enjoy with tortilla chips or whatever you want to dunk in there.

SERVES 8

PREP TIME: 10 minutes **TOTAL TIME:** 50 minutes

ARMADILLO CHEESY GARLIC BREAD

- **3 cups shredded mozzarella cheese**
- **1½ sticks (6 ounces) butter, at room temperature**
- **½ cup mayonnaise**
- **1½ cups finely grated Parmigiano-Reggiano cheese**
- **2 tablespoons finely minced garlic (about 4 cloves)**
- **1 teaspoon red pepper flakes**
- **1 teaspoon kosher salt**
- **1 teaspoon freshly ground black pepper**
- **1-pound round loaf French bread**

I'm having trouble even writing about this because it's the most obvious sell in the world. I mean look at it!! Every single time I make it, there are five hands reaching for a piece and this is before it even hits the table. Watching people ooh and aah over each cheese stretch makes my icy heart melt. It is excessive in the best way possible—a lot of cheese, a lot of garlic. Crispy and yet perfectly pillow-like inside. I would tell you to serve it hot, but it won't last long enough to even cool down. Me wanty now.

Preheat the oven to 400°F.

In a bowl, combine the mozzarella, butter, mayo, Parm, garlic, red pepper flakes, salt, and black pepper. Using a serrated knife, cut the bread in a crosshatch pattern, making cuts 2 inches apart and taking care not to cut through the bottom of the bread.

Place the bread on a large sheet of foil on a baking sheet. Stuff most of the cheese mixture into all of the cracks in the bread. Slather the remainder over the top of the bread. Coat another sheet of foil with cooking spray and lay spray-side down on the top of the loaf. Crimp the two pieces together to seal the bread in foil.

Bake for 20 minutes, then reduce the oven temperature to 375°F. Remove the top sheet of foil and bake until the top gets golden and the cheese is super melty, 15 to 20 minutes longer.

SH*T ON TOAST

1. **TOMATO/HERBED CHEESE:** Make a batch of the Garlic Herb Cheese (from the Prosciutto-Wrapped Stuffed Chicken Breasts, page 232), but use half the garlic. Spread on toasts, then pile with sliced tomatoes and chopped cilantro.
2. **FIG/RICOTTA/HONEY/SALAMI/BLACK PEPPER:** Top 1 slice of toasted bread with 2 tablespoons fresh ricotta, 2 to 3 thin slices salami or soppressata, and a quarter of a fig. Drizzle with honey, a big pinch of thyme leaves, and a grind of freshly cracked pepper.
3. **MOM'S STEAK:** Top a toast point with a slice of leftover steak and a few serious drops of Pepper's Red Hot Pepper Sauce (page 107), half a cherry tomato, and a few shreds of scallion.
4. **CRAB/BUTTER/JALAPEÑO:** In a small saucepan, heat 2 tablespoons butter over medium heat. When it foams, add 1 finely chopped shallot and cook until translucent, about 2 minutes. Add 1 seeded, finely chopped jalapeño and ½ pound lump crabmeat, and warm through, 1 minute. Season with salt and pepper and pile on toasts.
5. **AVOCADO/PROSCIUTTO/TOMATO/RED ONION:** Mash an avocado with salt, pepper, and lime juice. Spread thickly on whole wheat toasts, then top with tomato slices, prosciutto, shaved red onion, salt, pepper, and a pinch of red pepper flakes. Breakfast of champions!
6. **RASPBERRY/TALEGGIO:** In a small saucepan, simmer 2 cups raspberries with ½ cup sugar for 15 minutes, mashing and stirring until thickened and the bubbling has calmed down. Stir in 2 tablespoons lemon juice and let cool. (Hey, you just made raspberry jam! Keep it in the fridge.) Top with a little chunk of taleggio or Brie and broil until the cheese is halfway melted. Grate a little lemon zest over the top.
7. **CINNAMON TOAST/DARK CHOCOLATE:** In a bowl, mix together 1 stick (4 ounces) softened butter, ¼ cup sugar, 2 teaspoons ground cinnamon, and a pinch of salt. Spread on bread and toast in a 350°F oven until browned and toasty, about 10 minutes. Let cool for 2 minutes, then shave dark chocolate on top.
8. **SALTED PEANUT BUTTER/CARAMEL/GRAPES:** Mix equal parts creamy peanut butter and jarred caramel sauce. Spread on toasts, top with chopped salted peanuts and sliced grapes. Finish with flaky sea salt.

5

8

6

4

PREP TIME: 5 minutes **TOTAL TIME:** 5 to 25 minutes

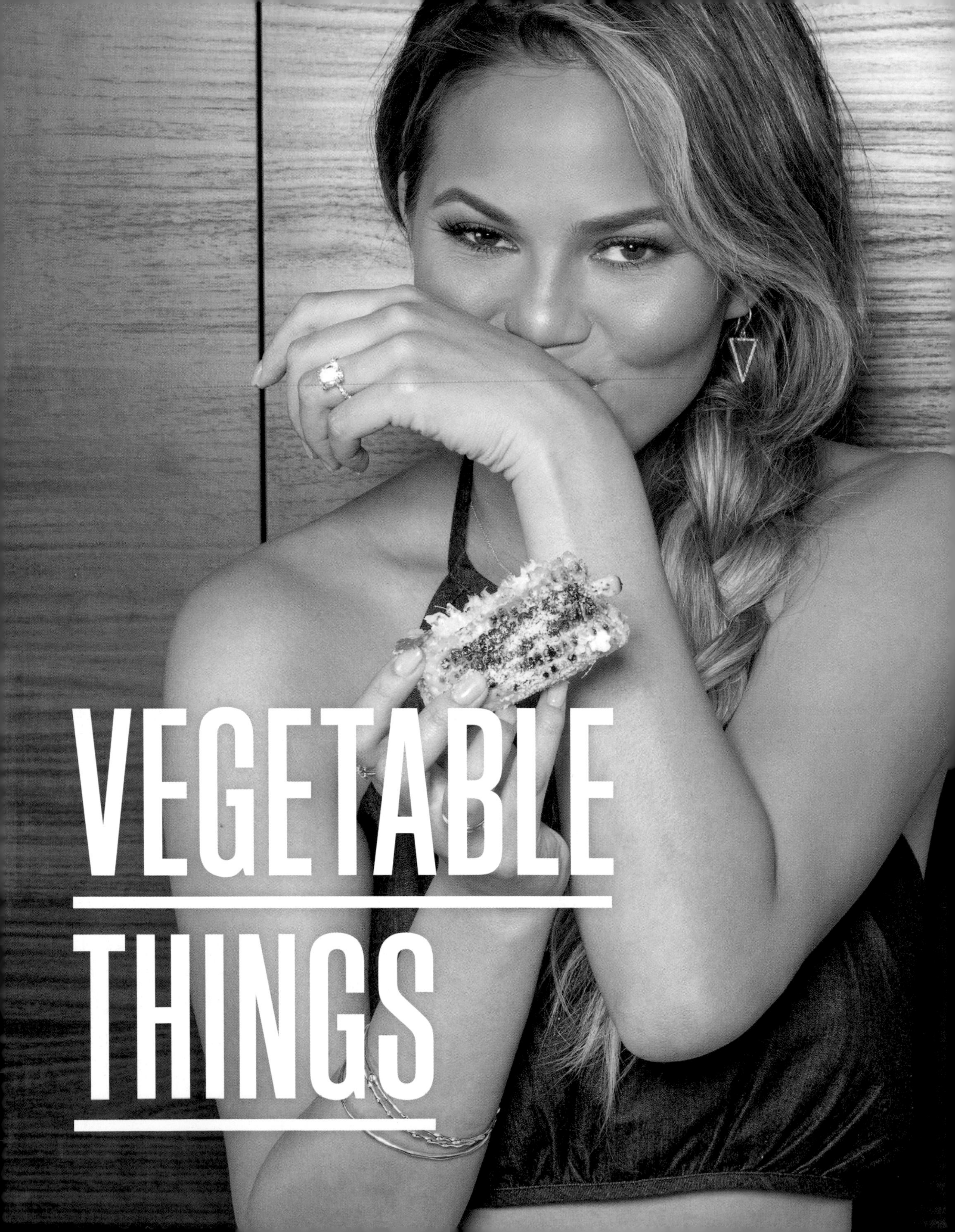

VEGETABLE THINGS

Opposite: Mexican Street Corn
(PAGE 167)

SERVES 4

PREP TIME: 20 minutes **TOTAL TIME:** 30 minutes

BUTTERY GLAZED GREEN BEANS

¼ cup sugar
Kosher salt
1 pound green beans, trimmed
2 tablespoons unsalted butter
¼ teaspoon black pepper
¼ cup slivered almonds, lightly toasted

I'm willing to bet you have never had green beans like this before. I'm actually willing to say these will be the best freaking green beans you've ever had in your life.

These beans have been through more trial and error than I'm OK with admitting, but even the errors were hysterical. The first attempt left us with some kind of Whole Foods-candy-aisle-looking monstrosity: green beans clumped together by chewy strands of sugar syrup. There were approximately 8 seconds of disappointment followed by 30 minutes of consuming the entire lot. If we were going for candy beans, YES, we nailed it. But no. I wanted lightly sweet and buttery, bright and plump beanies to complement all my savory little main babies. But note to self . . . next book: candy beans.

In a large skillet with a tight-fitting lid, combine 1 cup water, the sugar, and 1 teaspoon salt and bring to a boil, stirring until the sugar is dissolved. Add the green beans, cover, and cook over medium-high heat until the sugar water begins to reduce, 7 to 9 minutes. Uncover and continue to cook, tossing the beans, until the sugar reduces to a very light syrup and the beans are no longer crisp but somehow miraculously aren't mushy, making sure it doesn't burn (add a splash of water if necessary), 7 to 9 minutes.

Transfer to a serving dish and top with the butter and pepper. Season to taste with more salt. Garnish with the almonds.

MAKES 6 CUPS / SERVES 8

PREP TIME: 10 minutes **TOTAL TIME:** 30 minutes

CAULIFLOWER MASH
WITH ROASTED GARLIC AND RICOTTA

- Kosher salt
- 1 large head cauliflower, broken into florets
- 1 cup ricotta cheese
- 4 tablespoons (½ stick) butter
- 3 tablespoons Roasted Garlic (recipe follows), plus more for garnish
- 2 tablespoons Roasted Garlic Oil (recipe follows)
- Freshly ground black pepper

Whenever anyone asks me what my diet secret is, I say one word: trickery. So much of my life is tricking myself into thinking I am getting that so-desired dish that I can't actually have at the moment.

Potatoes are my heart and soul. I get a physical and emotional rush when potatoes are making their way down my gullet. Sometimes I can't have potatoes and so I mash cauliflower instead. But dare I say I almost prefer these fake-ass mashed potatoes? Actually, you know what, they are different and I need them both. They are my sister wives. My creamy, garlic sister wives.

Plus they go with absolutely everything, or you can eat them solo, which is kind of weird but who am I to judge?

Bring a large pot of water to a boil and salt it until it tastes good. Add the cauliflower and cook until you can easily pierce it with a fork, 15 to 20 minutes. Drain it in a colander, then spread the cauliflower out on a paper towel to soak up extra moisture (you want it to be as dry as possible).

Working in batches, place the cauliflower in a food processor with the ricotta, butter, roasted garlic, garlic oil, ¼ teaspoon pepper, and 1 teaspoon salt and process until almost smooth but some chunks remain, 20 to 30 seconds. Season to taste with more salt and pepper. Garnish with more cloves of roasted garlic and serve warm.

roasted garlic and roasted garlic oil

MAKES 30 TO 40 CLOVES and 2 CUPS OIL

PREP TIME: 5 minutes **TOTAL TIME:** 2 hours

2¼ cups olive oil
30 large or 40 medium cloves garlic, peeled

In a small saucepan, combine the oil and garlic. Set over medium-low heat and don't turn it any higher, you impatient people! The oil will heat up slowly and the garlic will start to sort of fizz and sizzle after 10 to 15 minutes. Continue to cook the garlic until it slowly turns golden brown but stays really soft, 30 to 40 minutes longer (if it gets dark or starts to develop a bubbly, sort of hard outer layer, turn the heat down).

Remove from the heat and let the garlic sit in the oil on the counter for another hour or two, or up to 24. Strain the garlic cloves from the oil and keep them refrigerated separately in tightly sealed containers. Before using the oil, let it come to room temperature or run the jar under warm water for 1 minute to liquefy.

SERVES 4 TO 6

PREP TIME: 15 minutes **TOTAL TIME:** 1 hour

THYME-ROASTED CARROTS

1½ pounds medium carrots
3 tablespoons extra-virgin olive oil
1 teaspoon kosher salt
¼ teaspoon freshly ground black pepper
6 thyme sprigs

These are carrots, and they are roasted with thyme. They are simple, and they are divine. Made any other way, would just be a crime. I hope you've enjoyed, my thyme carrot rhyme.

They are also very, very easy to make. If you can't make these you should just go ahead and return this book. Not being able to cook at all isn't SO bad—you can turn your kitchen into an extra bedroom!

Preheat the oven to 400°F. Line a large rimmed baking sheet with foil.

Peel the carrots. If they have tops, trim them, leaving 1 inch of the greens on. Slice any fatter carrots (thicker than 1 inch) in half lengthwise. Leave the smaller ones whole.

Arrange the carrots on the baking sheet. Drizzle with the oil and sprinkle with the salt and pepper. Jiggle the pan so the oil, salt, and pepper coat the carrots on all sides. Scatter the thyme sprigs among the carrots and roast until the undersides are golden and caramelized, 30 to 40 minutes. If they can't be easily pierced with a fork yet, shake the carrots and continue to roast 5 to 10 minutes longer.

SERVES 4 TO 6

PREP TIME: 10 minutes **TOTAL TIME:** 45 minutes

ROASTED MUSHROOMS

- 1 stick (4 ounces) unsalted butter, melted
- ¼ cup extra-virgin olive oil
- 2 tablespoons minced garlic (about 3 cloves)
- 2 tablespoons chopped fresh thyme
- 2 teaspoons kosher salt
- 1 teaspoon freshly ground black pepper
- 1 pound white mushrooms, trimmed and cleaned
- 1 pound cremini mushrooms, trimmed and cleaned

If I were ever, ever to become a vegetarian, I am absolutely positive I would survive mainly off mushrooms. Mushrooms are my secret lover, my mister-ess, the unspoken love of my food life. Juicy and meaty, these are the gold standard for roasted mushrooms.

Preheat the oven to 425°F.

In a large bowl, combine the melted butter, oil, garlic, thyme, salt, and pepper. Add the white and cremini mushrooms and toss to coat. Pour the mushrooms onto a large rimmed baking sheet and roast, shaking occasionally, until shriveled but still really juicy, 30 to 45 minutes (depending on the size of your mushrooms).

MAKES 8 PIECES / SERVES 4 TO 8

PREP TIME: 10 minutes **TOTAL TIME:** 20 minutes

MEXICAN STREET CORN

¾ cup finely grated Parmigiano-Reggiano cheese

¾ cup crumbled cotija cheese (it's like Mexican feta!)

½ teaspoon freshly ground black pepper

4 ears corn, husked and halved

1 tablespoon vegetable oil

1 teaspoon kosher salt

2 tablespoons mayonnaise

Cayenne pepper

¼ cup chopped fresh cilantro leaves

1 lime, cut into 8 wedges

Ohhhhhhhh my god I am like freaking Cookie Monster when it comes to Mexican street corn. I get rabid. I completely stop caring about my physical appearance or bodily noises, the entire world around me disappears. My eyes point in different directions, nose full of cotija cheese, chunks of corn taking permanent residence in my purchased pearly whites. And I don't even care. The only thing I care about is how. I can consume. More corn.

This is a BBQ/sporting event/family reunion dinner/Grandpa's wake/release from prison party must. Corn made any other way is a waste of dental floss.

Preheat a large cast-iron skillet over high heat. On a plate, combine the Parm, cotija, and black pepper.

Use a brush to coat the pieces of corn with oil, or get them greasy with your hands. Season with the salt and lay as many pieces as will fit comfortably in the skillet. Cook, turning every 2 minutes, until some bits are blackened and the corn is cooked, about 8 minutes total.

Working quickly, brush each piece with a thin layer of mayonnaise, then roll the corn in the cheese mixture and sprinkle with cayenne to taste. Put all the cheesy corn on a platter, garnish with the cilantro, and serve with lime wedges for squeezing.

SERVES 4 TO 6

PREP TIME: 15 minutes **TOTAL TIME:** 45 minutes

BALSAMIC GLAZED BRUSSELS SPROUTS

WITH BACON, CRANBERRIES, WALNUTS, AND BLUE CHEESE

- **1½ pounds Brussels sprouts, trimmed and halved lengthwise**
- **15 cloves garlic, peeled**
- **¼ cup olive oil**
- **Kosher salt and freshly ground black pepper**
- **¼ cup Honey-Balsamic Glaze (recipe follows)**
- **4 slices bacon, cooked and crumbled (see Note)**
- **½ cup chopped toasted walnuts**
- **¼ cup dried cranberries**
- **¼ cup crumbled blue cheese**

We are one Brussels sprouts–loving family. So for us, this dish is basically something *already* great *with* a f*cking delicious sweet glaze *and* frolicking with other delicious, great things. For someone who despises Brussels sprouts, it's a bunch of sprouts covered in delicious, great things. Honestly both these scenarios seem, well, great. And those people will never, ever be able to say they despise Brusselsssssss sprouts ever, ever again.

Preheat the oven to 450°F.

In a bowl, toss together the Brussels sprouts, garlic, olive oil, 2 teaspoons salt, and 1 teaspoon pepper. Dump onto a large baking sheet, spreading them around so everything is in one layer. Roast until the undersides get browned and crisp, about 20 minutes. Remove from the oven, toss to release the undersides, and return to the oven to finish roasting, until some of the sprouts are charred and the garlic cloves are tender, about 10 minutes longer.

Transfer to a platter and season to taste with more salt and pepper. Drizzle with the balsamic glaze, then scatter the bacon, walnuts, cranberries, and blue cheese all over the top.

note

The best way to cook bacon is on a baking sheet, the way I do it for Garlic-Roasted Bacon (page 17) . . . minus the garlic.

honey-balsamic glaze

MAKES ¾ CUP

TOTAL TIME: 20 minutes

1 cup balsamic vinegar
½ cup honey

In the smallest saucepan you have, combine the vinegar and honey and bring to a boil, then reduce the heat and simmer until the glaze reduces by half and is thick and small and bubbles form on the entire surface of the liquid, about 20 minutes. Remove from the heat and let cool to room temperature. This will keep indefinitely in the fridge in an airtight container; warm slightly before using.

SERVES 8 TO 10

PREP TIME: 20 minutes **TOTAL TIME:** 1 hour 15 minutes

HAM AND CHEESE GREEN BEAN CASSEROLE

- **Butter, for greasing the baking dish**
- **4 cups low-sodium chicken broth or water**
- **1 pound green beans, trimmed and cut into 2-inch lengths**
- **2 (10.75-ounce) cans condensed cream of mushroom soup**
- **¾ cup half-and-half**
- **1 teaspoon garlic powder**
- **½ teaspoon kosher salt**
- **½ teaspoon freshly ground black pepper**
- **½ pound ham, diced**
- **½ cup diced onion**
- **2½ cups shredded cheddar cheese**
- **1 cup canned French fried onions**

I know. A lot of my recipes involve ham. I am not apologizing for it! I WILL, however, say that I will never put pork in something just for the fun of it—it has to enhance the entire dish. It just so happens that pork enhances most dishes, OK!?

I had been making the same green bean casserole for years. It was kind of just a dish that you needed to have at holidays because it fits the bill. But I grew tired of it just being alive but not LIVING, you know?? So I needed to add ham. I am being serious. I am not high.

Aside from the ham, this is a relatively traditional, homey, crowd-pleasing dish. Write the recipe on a notecard, burn the edges and pretend it's your great-great-grandmother's recipe. No one will doubt you!

Preheat the oven to 350°F. Butter a 10 × 12-inch baking dish.

In a medium saucepan, bring the chicken broth to a boil. Add the green beans and cook until tender-crisp, 5 to 6 minutes. Drain and save the chicken broth for another use.

In a large bowl, whisk together the soup, half-and-half, garlic powder, salt, and pepper. Stir in the green beans, ham, onion, 2 cups of the cheddar, and ¾ cup of the fried onions.

Pour the casserole mixture into the baking dish. Sprinkle with the remaining ½ cup cheddar and bake until bubbling and crusty, about 40 minutes, adding the remaining ¼ cup onions during the last 10 minutes of baking. Remove from the oven, let sit for 5 minutes, and serve.

SERVES 4

PREP TIME: 15 minutes **TOTAL TIME:** 40 minutes

ZUCCHINI FRIES

- **1¼ cups all-purpose flour**
- **½ teaspoon cayenne pepper**
- **Kosher salt and freshly ground black pepper**
- **3 eggs**
- **1 cup panko bread crumbs (these are super-dry Japanese bread crumbs that make things mega crispy)**
- **1¼ cups finely grated Parmigiano-Reggiano cheese**
- **3 tablespoons olive oil**
- **4 small zucchini (1 pound), trimmed and quartered lengthwise, or 2 medium zucchini, halved crosswise and quartered lengthwise**
- **Sriracha Caesar Dressing (page 65) or Honey-Mustard Ranch Dressing (from Cobb Salad, page 72)**

Thick cut and perfectly crunchy *annnnnnd baked,* these guys will seriously make you forget you're being kinda a little bit somewhat semihealthy. Which is why we must dip them in mayo. We can't throw off the universe's balance/equilibrium thing. It's a science thing. Don't question it. (See photograph, page 211.)

Preheat the oven to 425°F.

In a wide, shallow bowl, combine the flour, cayenne, 2 teaspoons salt, and ½ teaspoon black pepper. In another wide, shallow bowl, whisk the eggs to combine. In a third bowl, stir together the panko, Parm, and olive oil with a fork until incorporated.

One at a time, roll the zucchini in the flour mixture. Shake off the excess, then dip in the egg, allowing the excess to drip back into the bowl. Dip in the panko coating, pressing on all sides to coat (especially the green, rounded side, which can be slippery—just make sure the crumbs are pressed in there!), and arrange on a baking sheet.

Bake until golden, 20 to 25 minutes. Season to taste with salt and pepper.

Serve with one of the dressings as a dipping sauce.

SERVES 4

PREP TIME: 10 minutes **TOTAL TIME:** 25 minutes

CHARRED AND GARLICKY BROCCOLI

- **3 tablespoons Roasted Garlic Oil (page 163) or olive oil**
- **2 medium heads broccoli, cut into florets**
- **¼ teaspoon red pepper flakes**
- **1 teaspoon kosher salt**
- **¼ teaspoon freshly ground black pepper**
- **¼ cup low sodium chicken or vegetable broth**
- **¼ cup Roasted Garlic (page 163)**
- **½ cup Cheesy Garlic Bread Crumbs (page 92)**
- **¼ cup finely grated Parmigiano-Reggiano cheese**

I have no doubt John's love for broccoli rivals his love for me. But good lord, I am so freaking bored when I make it that I might just let her have him.

I mean, I WAS bored. Until I realized that sprinkling my go-to cheesy garlic bread crumbs onto big hunks of broccoli is basically like Tinkerbell spreading her fairy dust—or whoever the hell did that. Listen, the first movie I saw in a theater was *Monster's Ball*, so I'm not exactly up on my kid sh*t.

Long story short (not really, I just have nothing left to write), this is the only way we will do broccoli in the Teigen-Stephens household now. Bye-bye boring broccoli!

Heat a 12-inch skillet with a tight-fitting lid over medium-high heat. Add the oil and when it's shimmering-hot, add the broccoli and red pepper flakes and season with the salt and pepper. Cook, turning the broccoli to sear evenly, until lightly charred, 3 to 4 minutes. Add the broth and roasted garlic, then cover and cook until the broccoli is softened, about 5 minutes longer.

Transfer to a serving platter, then top with the cheesy garlic bread crumbs and the Parm.

THINGS THAT INTIMIDATE PEOPLE BUT SHOULDN'T

// *Opposite:* Sweet Chili and Mustard-Glazed Salmon Fillets (PAGE 189)

SERVES 2 AS A MAIN COURSE or 4 AS AN APPETIZER

PREP TIME: 25 minutes **TOTAL TIME:** 45 minutes

SWEET POTATO GNOCCHI WITH BROWN BUTTER AND SAGE

My Dough Terror is well documented—I get night sweats thinking about having to combine flour, water, and salt into something that is actually edible. But this dough, my friends, is different. Yes, it's got all the telltale signs of an epic kitchen fail, but the addition of ricotta cheese makes it just forgiving enough that you might actually want to make gnocchi again—for other people, no less. The secret is to bring the dough together, and then to not overwork the situation (nothing's worse than someone trying too hard). After a quick boil, toast the gnocchi in brown butter and sage, shower them in cheese, and take a picture to prove to everyone that you really did pull off these fluffy orange pasta pillows yourself.

for the **GNOCCHI**

- 1 pound sweet potato (about 1 large)
- ⅓ cup whole-milk ricotta cheese
- ½ teaspoon freshly ground black pepper
- Kosher salt
- ¾ cup all-purpose flour, plus more if necessary

MAKE THE GNOCCHI: Pierce the sweet potato all over with a fork, wrap in a damp paper towel, and microwave on high until it is very soft, 12 to 13 minutes.

When the sweet potato is cool enough to handle, peel it and mash the flesh with a potato masher or ricer in a medium bowl until smooth. Stir in the ricotta, pepper, and 1 teaspoon salt, then scatter the flour into the mixture. Mix with a fork until a doughy mixture forms that's loose and shaggy but doesn't stick to the sides of the bowl; if necessary, add more flour, 1 tablespoon at a time.

In a large pasta pot, bring a gallon of water to a boil over high heat and salt it until it tastes good.

Flour your work surface and dump the dough onto it. Flour your hands and gently knead the dough 10 times—by folding the dough in half, pressing gently with the heel of your hand, and turning it 90 degrees each time —until it is no longer sticky. Add sprinkles of flour when necessary, but the less flour you use, the more tender the gnocchi will be.

// *recipe continues*

for the
SAUCE

- **1 stick (4 ounces) unsalted butter**
- **¼ cup torn fresh sage leaves**
- **½ cup finely grated Parmigiano-Reggiano cheese, plus more for garnish**
- **Kosher salt and freshly ground black pepper**

Divide the dough into 3 equal pieces and gently roll them into balls. On a floured surface, using your hands, roll one ball of dough into a 12-inch-long, 1-inch-thick log. Use a paring knife to cut the dough crosswise into twelve 1-inch pieces. Repeat with the remaining dough balls to form about 36 gnocchi.

Drop the gnocchi into the boiling water, stirring after about 1 minute to ensure they aren't sticking to the bottom of the pot, and cook until they float to the surface for a few seconds and are tender-firm, 4 to 5 minutes.

MEANWHILE, MAKE THE SAUCE: While the gnocchi are cooking, in a large skillet, melt the butter over medium heat. When the foam subsides, add the sage and cook until the sage is crispy and the butter is browned, about 3 minutes.

Drain the gnocchi (don't rinse it) and add it to the skillet. Toss to coat in the butter, add the Parm, and season to taste with salt and pepper.

Divide among bowls and garnish with more Parm.

feel the dough

Gnocchi dough doesn't have to give you nightmares. The texture you want is like softened Toll House cookie dough. So if your dough is too sticky, add a little flour at a time, but don't knead it too hard—that will make the gnocchi tough little cookies.

SERVES 2 AS A MAIN COURSE or 4 AS AN APPETIZER

PREP TIME: 35 minutes **TOTAL TIME:** 1 hour 30 minutes

RISOTTO WITH PORCINI MUSHROOMS AND PEAS

Every time we go out for Italian, I mentally choose the burrata starter, branzino, and some sort of berries and cream formation for dessert because it's fruit and fruit is healthy and the cream is milk and milk is basically mother nature juice.

Then the demon with the specials of course announces a risotto. And I must have it. I order it. This happens, without fail, every single time. (And that, my friends, is the story of how I have never booked a New York Fashion Week show.)

But I used to never make it at home, because thanks to Gordon Ramsay, who thinks everyone in the entire universe except him makes garbage risotto, making it *kinnnnnnnda* scared the crap out of me. I put a pan on the stove, and I truly thought he would pop out of f*cking nowhere, scream that my risotto is sh*t, then call me a moon-faced baby for crying.

But once you know the technique, you know everything. It really is one of those intimidating dishes you need not be threatened by. You just keep a pot of simmering broth going on the back burner, add it a little at a time, stir stir stir, and don't get distracted by reality TV or your dog drinking your vodka soda or your Thai Mom trying to sneak fish sauce into your Italian food. Pay attention, stir often, and you will be risotto golden.

2 ounces dried porcini mushrooms
2 cups warm water
3 cups low-sodium chicken or vegetable broth
3 tablespoons unsalted butter
1 shallot or ¼ small onion, finely chopped
1 cup Arborio rice
½ cup dry white wine
1 teaspoon kosher salt
½ cup frozen peas, thawed
1 cup shredded Parmigiano-Reggiano cheese, plus more for garnish
Freshly ground black pepper

Place the porcinis and warm water in a bowl and soak until soft, at least 1 hour and up to 4 hours. Remove the mushrooms, squeeze them so the liquid drips back into the bowl, and strain the liquid through a piece of cheesecloth or a very fine strainer. Remove any tough pieces of rehydrated mushroom stems, finely chop the mushrooms, and set them aside.

Transfer the strained soaking liquid to a medium saucepan, leaving behind any grit in the bottom of the bowl, and add the chicken broth. Warm the broth over medium-low heat until steaming and keep warm on a back burner.

In another medium saucepan, heat 2 tablespoons of the butter over medium heat. Add the shallot and cook, stirring, until translucent but not browned, about 5 minutes. Add the rice and cook, stirring, for 2 minutes. Add the wine and salt, increase the heat to medium-high, and boil until the wine is mostly evaporated, 2 to 3 minutes.

// ***recipe continues***

Microplane
PATENT 5100506

Return the heat to medium and, using a ladle, add 1 cup of the broth to the rice and cook, stirring, until the broth is almost all absorbed. Keep adding ½ cup of broth at a time, waiting to add more until most of the broth in the pot is absorbed each time, and cook, stirring occasionally, until the rice is swollen and still very slightly firm in the middle, about 22 minutes total (you may be left with a little broth you don't use; traditionally the risotto should be a little loose and saucy, but how wet you want it is up to you).

Stir in the peas and cook just long enough to warm them through, then stir in the remaining 1 tablespoon butter, the Parm, and reserved chopped porcini.

Divide the risotto among bowls and garnish with pepper and a little more Parm.

the right rice

Risotto rice is typically short and round, meaning the opposite of Uncle Ben's long-and-skinny. It's also starchy, which is why the risotto gets all creamy when you cook it. In the store, look for Arborio or carnaroli varieties.

SERVES 2 TO 4

PREP TIME: 15 minutes **TOTAL TIME:** 30 minutes

PERFECT SEARED SCALLOPS WITH WARM CORN SALAD

Seared scallops were a dish I couldn't say no to at a restaurant, but making them at home?? Oh no no no, too fancy!!

How wrong I was. Once you know the tricks, you'll be impressing your friend or lover or friend you are secretly in love with in no time. What are those tricks, you ask? (1) Pat your scallops nice and dry with paper towels, so they caramelize in the pan, not steam. (2) Don't season until righhhhht before searing. (The salt brings more water out, which is the enemy of browning.) (3) Get your pan really hot and add oil before butter so your buttah don't burn. Four: DFWT!!! Don't f*ck with them! Resist the urge to nudge, flip, rub, lick, stroke, or poke.

And on top of a bed of sweet corn salad? This is how your scallop wanted to go out.

for the **WARM CORN SALAD**

- 2 tablespoons unsalted butter
- 1 (15-ounce) can corn kernels, drained, or 2 cups fresh kernels (from 3 large ears)
- ½ small red bell pepper, diced
- 1 scallion, thinly sliced
- Kosher salt and freshly ground black pepper

for the **SCALLOPS**

- 12 extra-large or 6 jumbo scallops (about 1 pound)
- 2 tablespoons light olive oil or canola oil
- 1 tablespoon unsalted butter
- Kosher salt and freshly ground black pepper

MAKE THE SALAD: In a large heavy skillet, heat the butter over medium heat. When it foams, add the corn, bell pepper, and scallion and sauté, tossing lightly, until cooked but still crisp, about 3 minutes. Season to taste with salt and black pepper and hold warm in the pan off the heat.

MAKE THE SCALLOPS: Pat the scallops dry with paper towels; if they're really fresh they should smell sweet and good and you shouldn't have to rinse them. Don't salt them yet—it makes the tops wet, so just hold your horses!

Heat a medium skillet (NOT nonstick) over medium-high heat for 2 minutes. It should be really hot but not screaming hot. Add 1 tablespoon of the oil, then add ½ tablespoon of the butter and swirl the pan (adding the oil first helps prevent the butter from burning). Sprinkle half of the scallops heavily with salt and pepper and add them to the skillet, seasoned-side down. DO NOT MOVE THEM! DO NOT TOUCH THEM! YOU WILL THANK ME! Cook the scallops until a crust forms, about 2 minutes. Pat the tops of the scallops down with a paper towel, season them heavily with salt and pepper, and flip the scallops. Cook another 1 to 1½ minutes max, until both sides are beautifully seared. Wipe out the skillet if it is too dark. Cook the remaining scallops in the same manner, using the remaining oil and butter.

Transfer to a plate and serve with the warm corn salad.

cutting corn

To cut fresh corn off the cob, stand the corn on its end, and shave the kernels off the sides with a sharp knife. Or you can lay it down on a cutting board, slice off one side of the kernels, and rotate the cob, scraping off the corners when you've gone all the way around. But hell, I love good canned corn, so I don't bother.

SERVES 2

PREP TIME: 20 minutes **TOTAL TIME:** 35 minutes

CHILE-GINGER PAPER-BAKED FISH

Somehow, this is THE fish recipe for people who either love fish or absolutely despise it. For the people who already love fish, the layers of ginger and garlic and spice create this crazy roller coaster of flavor that is, ahem, totally unique, thank you very much. For people who hate fish, those layers of flavor will open you up to a whole new world: a world where fish doesn't taste fishy. (Isn't that always the excuse? And guess what, STEAKS BE STEAKY.)

Baking it in paper is not only the ultimate show-off move, but it also ensures your fish is super juicy, in its own little aroma sauna. Gently tear open the top of the parchment or taped-together rolling papers and breathe in that goodness.

I would sit in that sauna.

// ***recipe continues***

- **1 large serrano or jalapeño pepper, seeded and chopped**
- **1 large red Fresno chile or another jalapeño pepper, seeded and chopped**
- **1 scallion, chopped**
- **1½ tablespoons minced garlic (about 2 cloves)**
- **4 (4-inch-long, ⅛-inch-thick) zucchini strips (from 1 zucchini)**
- **1 (12-ounce) cod fillet**
- **Kosher salt and freshly ground black pepper**
- **2 large shiitake mushroom caps, thinly sliced**
- **1-inch piece fresh ginger, peeled and cut into thin coins**
- **2 tablespoons canned coconut milk (preferably full-fat, but use light here if you must)**
- **1 tablespoon mirin**
- **1 teaspoon light soy sauce**
- **½ teaspoon toasted sesame oil**
- **½ teaspoon fresh lime juice**

Preheat the oven to 450°F.

Cut a 12 × 18-inch piece of parchment or foil. Fold the parchment in half (to make an 12 × 9-inch rectangle), trace a half-heart on it, and cut it out of the parchment with scissors. (Like you did in grade school to put on the family refrigerator.) (If you're using foil, butter the side of the foil the food will go on.)

In a bowl, combine the serrano and Fresno chiles, scallion, and garlic. Open up the parchment heart and place half the chile mixture in the center of one half. Arrange the zucchini slices on top to form a bed for the fish. (Lay them down at an angle so that they fit inside the paper heart.) Season the fish with salt and pepper and place on top of the zucchini. Cover the fish with the remaining chile mixture. Top with the shiitakes and the ginger coins.

In a small bowl, whisk together the coconut milk, mirin, soy sauce, sesame oil, lime juice, and a pinch of salt and pour the mixture on top of the fish.

Fold the other half of parchment heart over the fish. Starting from the round side, fold the edges of the parchment in toward the fish. Working as methodically as you can, keep folding the parchment over, all the way around the edge, creasing and sealing each fold; the key is to seal the liquid and fish inside the parchment. When you get to the pointy corner, fold it back toward the edge of the parchment to seal the package.

Place the package on a rimmed baking sheet and bake until the parchment puffs slightly and the fish is cooked through, 12 to 15 minutes. Rip open that parchment and serve that baby hot.

cooks' origami

Folding the fish in a heart-shaped piece of parchment is like origami for cooks. Basically, you're trying to create a seal around the fish so it steams up tender and flavorful. If you don't have parchment or don't feel like doing an art project, just seal the fish in a packet of foil, using a little extra foil so the food has room to steam.

SERVES 4

PREP TIME: 10 minutes **TOTAL TIME:** 15 minutes

SWEET CHILI AND MUSTARD-GLAZED SALMON FILLETS

Having grown up in Washington state, I have a love-hate relationship with salmon. Salmon was effing everywhere in every form. Smoked, poached, seared, in my face, up my stream, seriously you could not get away from salmon. And don't get me started on smoked breakfast salmon. Why would you do that to a bagel? WHY? I get angry just thinking about it.

Basically what I'm saying is that I have had salmon every which way and there is nothing that compares to this saucy little bastard. Sweet chili that caramelizes and bubbles and drenches your fillet in goodness?? Have fun with your lemon and one sprig of dill, I'll be over here.

- **4 (6-ounce) skin-on center-cut salmon fillets**
- **Kosher salt and freshly ground black pepper**
- **⅔ cup Thai sweet chili sauce**
- **2 tablespoons sambal oelek**
- **2 tablespoons large-grain mustard**

Position a rack 4 to 6 inches from the heating element and preheat the broiler.

Season the salmon all over with salt and pepper. In a small bowl, stir together the sweet chili sauce, sambal oelek, and mustard. Pour the mixture into a large cast-iron skillet. Set the skillet over medium-high heat and heat until the mixture begins to bubble. Lay the salmon, skin-side up, in that sauce. Cook until the salmon starts to turn pale pink on the outside, about 2 minutes, then move the skillet to the oven and broil until the skin crisps and the salmon is medium-rare, 3 to 4 minutes.

Remove the salmon from the oven and transfer the salmon to a serving platter. Return the skillet to the stove, add ¼ cup water, and cook over high heat, stirring and scraping, until the sauce thickens, about 2 minutes. Pour the sauce over the salmon and serve immediately.

lay off my salmon skin

To the Instahaters who called me out for the way I broil my salmon, don't knock it till you try it! Keeping the salmon flesh-side down all the way through keeps it moist as moist can be, and the broiler gets that skin crisp.

SERVES 2 TO 4

PREP TIME: 15 minutes **TOTAL TIME:** 35 minutes

HERBY, LEMONY, SPICY, GARLICKY ROASTED WHOLE FISH

People have such an aversion to food with faces, as if it was born without a face. If you're gonna enjoy something whose life was given up for your nourishment and enjoyment, I find it respectful to acknowledge that yes, that delicious, juicy thing indeed had a face. A delicious, fatty little face.

I eat and Instagram this dish quite often, and usually 25 percent of the comments are about being terrified of it. Anyone freaked out by it is solely freaked out by the head, but has never ever tried it. And you don't have to! Just go for that meaty, sexy body.

This is a household staple for us. Mom wakes up early like a kid on the first day of school just knowing it's the day we make this for lunch. I love sitting on our kitchen barstools and tossing out forks and picking at this guy like a bunch of scoundrels. It's food in its purest and most impressive form—and we can't live without it. Or the toothbrush we need after.

- **1 (2-pound) whole fish, such as branzino or striped bass, cleaned (but head on!)**
- **Kosher salt and freshly ground black pepper**
- **15 cloves garlic (yes, you read that right), mashed or finely minced**
- **2 teaspoons olive oil, plus more for drizzling**
- **½ teaspoon red pepper flakes**
- **1 lemon, sliced into rounds**
- **3 or 4 assorted herb sprigs (rosemary, thyme, sage, etc.)**
- **1 pound tomatoes, sliced or cut into wedges**

Preheat the oven to 450°F. Line a rimmed baking sheet with foil if you want easy cleanup.

Rinse the fish and pat it dry with paper towels. Place the fish on the baking sheet and season generously all over with salt and pepper. In a small bowl, combine the garlic, oil, and red pepper flakes, then rub it all over and inside the fish. Place the lemon rounds inside the cavity along with the herb sprigs. Arrange the tomatoes underneath and on top of the fish, then drizzle everything with some more olive oil.

Roast until the fish is flaky and opaque, about 20 minutes. Transfer to a serving platter and serve right away!

serving whole fish

To fillet the cooked fish, know that there is a spine running down the middle of the fish. Using a knife or a cake server, gently cut down the length of the spine to expose the bones. Then slip the tool under the flesh, and slide the half-fillet off the top half of the fish, before returning to the center line and sliding the bottom half-fillet off. If the fish is fully cooked, you should be able to lift the tail or head to take the whole spine out, leaving you with the rest of the fillet on the bottom. Do watch out for thin bones when you're eating, though.

SUPPER

MAKES ABOUT 15 PIECES/SERVES 4

PREP TIME: 30 minutes **TOTAL TIME:** 4 hours 45 minutes

PINEAPPLE-GRILLED SHORT RIBS

If you haven't had the meat candy that is Korean short ribs, let me tell you: YOU ARE MISSING OUT.

Thinly cut beef, swimming in a marinade of sweet brown sugar, sesame oil, and soy, grilled to caramelized perfection, good god. Then all that juicy goodness dripping down to the rice bed you've laid it on. I have no jokes for this dish. It's too good. And too too good if you have it with the Sweet and Salty Coconut Rice (page 83).

for the **RIBS**

- 2½ pounds flanken or kalbi-style short ribs (see Note)
- 1 teaspoon kosher salt
- 1 teaspoon freshly ground black pepper
- ½ cup (packed) dark brown sugar

for the **MARINADE**

- ½ cup light soy sauce
- ½ cup (packed) dark brown sugar
- ⅓ cup finely chopped garlic
- 2 tablespoons mirin
- 2 tablespoons finely grated fresh ginger
- 2 tablespoons minced fresh or canned pineapple
- 2 tablespoons finely grated yellow onion
- 1 tablespoon Sriracha
- ½ tablespoon sesame oil

for **SERVING**

- The rest of that pineapple, cored and sliced into half-moons
- ¼ cup chopped scallions
- Sweet and Salty Coconut Rice (page 83) or regular cooked rice

PREPARE THE RIBS: Place the ribs in a large baking dish or roasting pan and season them all over with the salt and pepper, then rub the brown sugar all over the ribs. Let them sit around in their sugary goodness (until the sugar dissolves on the surface of the ribs) for about 15 minutes.

MAKE THE MARINADE: In a bowl, combine the soy sauce, brown sugar, garlic, mirin, ginger, pineapple, onion, Sriracha, and sesame oil. Pour the marinade over the ribs, shaking the dish so the marinade gets all up in there. Cover and refrigerate for at least 4 hours, but 12 to 24 hours is better!

Remove the ribs from the fridge 30 minutes to 1 hour before cooking.

Remove the ribs from the marinade, letting the excess drain off, and pat dry with paper towels. Reserve the marinade. Preheat a grill or cast-iron skillet or griddle over high heat for 5 minutes. Grill the ribs until they get caramelized and are just cooked through, 3 to 4 minutes per side.

Throw the pineapple slices in the marinade to coat and grill them until caramelized, 2 to 3 minutes per side.

Serve the ribs and pineapple on a platter and garnish with chopped scallions. Serve rice alongside.

note

Flanken or kalbi short ribs are cut across the bone in thin pieces, with sections of bone attached. It should look like some kind of amazing avant garde fashion belt.

put mirin in food

Mirin is Japanese cooking wine. Mom uses mirin a lot cuz (a) it has alcohol in it and (b) it's a little sweet. But don't try to drink it in a pinch. No, really, you can't be that desperate. And it's got way too little alcohol, anyway.

SERVES 10 TO 12

PREP TIME: 1 hour **TOTAL TIME:** 3 hours 30 minutes

ZUCCHINI "LASAGNA" BOLOGNESE

for the **SAUCE (MAKES ABOUT 6 CUPS)**

- 3 tablespoons extra-virgin olive oil
- 1 tablespoon unsalted butter
- 1 large onion, finely chopped
- 1 large carrot, finely chopped
- 2 celery stalks, finely chopped
- 3 teaspoons kosher salt
- ½ teaspoon freshly ground black pepper
- 10 cloves garlic, chopped
- 1 fat rosemary sprig
- 1 teaspoon dried thyme or 2 teaspoons fresh
- 1 teaspoon dried oregano or 2 teaspoons fresh
- 1 teaspoon red pepper flakes
- ¾ pound ground pork
- ¾ pound ground beef
- 1 slice bacon, very finely chopped
- 1 cup red wine
- 1 cup milk
- 3 cups low-sodium chicken broth, plus more if needed
- 1 (28-ounce) can diced tomatoes
- 2 cups (loosely packed) basil leaves, shredded

Tell me about the last time you had bad lasagna. Think long and hard. It's impossible. Because there is absolutely no such thing as bad lasagna. But oh, there IS such a thing as great lasagna. The kind of lasagna you order so often that the waiter knows exactly how you want it done. For me, at Frank's, one of my favorite NYC Italian restaurants, it's their Lasagne Verdi, cooked well done, bubbling and crispy-edged. Another is the 100-Layer Lasagna from Mario Batali's Del Posto in NYC. Both beyond anything I could ever replicate.

If I can have carbs, I'll go to the greats. If I can't, at least I know what I love in a Bolognese sauce. So for now, until the scantily clad days are long behind me, I'll try to stick to the low-carb blessing that is my slow-cooked, ultra-savory meat sauce on roasted zucchini "noodles."

MAKE THE SAUCE: In a soup pot, heat the oil and butter over medium-low heat. Add the onion, carrot, celery, 1 teaspoon of the salt, and the pepper and cook, stirring, until softened but not browned, 12 to 13 minutes. Add the garlic, rosemary, thyme, oregano, and red pepper flakes and cook 2 minutes longer. Add the pork, beef, bacon, and 1 of the teaspoon salt. Increase the heat to medium-high and cook, breaking the meat up with a wooden spoon, until no longer pink, about 6 minutes. Add the wine and cook until most of the liquid evaporates, about 2 minutes. Add the milk, stirring, and cook 1 minute more. Add the broth, tomatoes, basil, and remaining 1 teaspoon salt. Bring to a boil, reduce the

// *recipe continues*

for the **ZUCCHINI "NOODLES"**

- **6 large zucchini (the longer the better), trimmed and sliced into long ¼-inch-thick strips**
- **2 teaspoons kosher salt**
- **2 tablespoons extra-virgin olive oil**

for the **FILLING**

- **1 (15-ounce) container whole-milk ricotta cheese**
- **1¾ cups shredded whole-milk mozzarella cheese**
- **1¾ cups finely shredded Parmigiano-Reggiano cheese**
- **1 large egg**
- **1 teaspoon kosher salt**
- **½ teaspoon red pepper flakes**
- **¼ teaspoon freshly ground black pepper**
- **1½ cups (loosely packed) basil leaves, shredded**

heat, and simmer until the sauce thickens and reduces, 1 hour to 1 hour 30 minutes, adding more broth if the sauce gets too dry (but you don't want it TOO liquidy! It should be a lot of meat, and a nice coating of thick yummy liquid).

ROAST THE ZUCCHINI "NOODLES": Arrange all of the zucchini strips in a single layer on 2 rimmed baking sheets and sprinkle one side with 1 teaspoon of the salt. Flip the zucchini and sprinkle with the remaining 1 teaspoon salt. Let some of the water come out of the zucchini for about 30 minutes. Pour off the water, then pat both sides of the zucchini dry with paper towels.

Preheat the oven to 425°F.

Brush the zucchini with the oil and roast until it loses half its thickness and some of the pieces get browned underneath (some will, some won't, but they should all be pretty soft), 25 to 30 minutes. Remove from the oven and cool.

MAKE THE FILLING: In a large bowl, combine the ricotta, 1 cup of the mozzarella, 1 cup of the Parm, the egg, salt, red pepper flakes, black pepper, and ½ cup of the basil.

BUILD AND BAKE THE LASAGNA: Preheat the oven to 350°F.

Spread 1 cup of the sauce on the bottom of a 9 × 13-inch lasagna pan. Arrange one layer of roasted zucchini on top of the sauce. Top with another cup of sauce, then dot with 1 cup of the cheese filling, and sprinkle with ¼ cup each of the basil, Parm, and mozzarella. Repeat with the zucchini, sauce, cheese filling, basil, Parm, and mozzarella two more times. Top the lasagna with the last layer of cheese filling, dolloping it all over the top. (Extra sauce keeps, refrigerated, for 1 week.)

Bake until the lasagna is bubbling and the top is golden, 40 to 45 minutes. Top with the remaining basil.

SERVES 4

PREP TIME: 10 minutes **TOTAL TIME:** 20 minutes

CAPON'S CHRISSY BURGER

AND ONION RINGS

for **CHRISSY'S SPECIAL SAUCE**

- ⅓ cup mayonnaise
- 2 tablespoons ketchup
- 2 tablespoons Cholula hot sauce
- 3 tablespoons chopped pickles

for the **PATTIES**

- 1½ pounds of the best, fattiest hamburger meat you can find (NOT lean; at least an 80/20 blend)
- 1½ teaspoons kosher salt
- 1½ teaspoons freshly ground black pepper
- 8 teaspoons Dijon mustard

for **ASSEMBLY**

- 4 hamburger buns of your choice (brioche, pretzel, potato, etc.)
- 4 lettuce leaves
- 4 big beefsteak tomato slices
- 4 slices American cheese
- 4 slices bacon, cooked to crisp
- Onion Rings (recipe follows)

If I'm in NYC and have a free afternoon, you can bet your ass that I am at Lure Fishbar in SoHo. Chef Josh Capon is not only a dear friend of mine, but he is also the man behind my absolute favorite burger in America. I mean the guy has won awards for it, including a belt only to be rivaled by WWE wrestlers. Not to mention we both have a love for American cheese that we refuse to be ashamed of. This burger is layer upon layer of mustard-seared perfection and topped with his signature onion ring. I LOVE it lettuce-wrapped at Lure, but, like everything, it's still better with carbs. We are all insanely lucky to have his award-winning recipe grace the pages of this book!

MAKE CHRISSY'S SPECIAL SAUCE: In a bowl, stir together the mayo, ketchup, Cholula, and pickles.

MAKE THE PATTIES: In a bowl, using your hands, gently combine the meat with the salt and pepper and gently form the meat into 4 patties (don't smash and press too hard; make nice to the burgers). Smear 2 teaspoons of the Dijon on top of each patty.

Heat a griddle or cast-iron skillet over medium-high heat and when very hot, cook the burgers, mustard-side up, for 3 minutes. Flip the burgers and cook 3 minutes more for medium-rare, 4 minutes for medium (the Dijon side will have developed a delicious caramelized sort of crust).

ASSEMBLE THE BURGERS: Lightly toast the buns. Spread a good amount of the special sauce on the bottom of each bun, then top with a lettuce leaf and a slice of tomato. Place a cooked burger on each bun, then top with a slice of cheese, a piece of bacon, and more sauce. Close the burger and serve with onion rings, or if your mouth is really wide, jam an onion ring right onto the burger itself.

onion rings

SERVES 4 TO 6

PREP TIME: 15 minutes
TOTAL TIME: 30 minutes

- ½ cup vegetable oil, plus more for frying
- 2 cups cornstarch
- 1¼ cups all-purpose flour
- 2 teaspoons paprika
- 1 teaspoon freshly ground black pepper
- ½ teaspoon garlic powder
- ¼ teaspoon cayenne pepper
- Kosher salt
- ½ cup dry white wine
- ½ cup beer
- 2 jumbo sweet or yellow onions

These are shockingly good both hot and at room temperature.

Fill a big pot with 4 inches of vegetable oil and heat the oil over medium-high heat until a small strand of the onion ring batter browns and crisps pretty fast when dropped into the oil (about 15 seconds). (If you're using a thermometer, I'm proud of you. Make it read 350°F.)

While the oil is heating, in a large bowl, whisk together the cornstarch, flour, paprika, black pepper, garlic powder, cayenne, and ½ tablespoon salt. Whisk in 1 cup water, the ½ cup vegetable oil, wine, and beer until smooth and thick.

Slice the onions crosswise into ¾-inch-thick rounds, then separate the rounds into rings.

When the oil is ready, dip the rings into the batter with tongs, a few at a time, pull them out, let a bit of the excess batter drip off, then fry them until golden and crispy, about 3 minutes (flip them once midway through frying). Only fry as many rings as will fit comfortably in the oil; they should have enough room to float around a bit. Drain on paper towels and season with salt.

SERVES 6

PREP TIME: 20 minutes **TOTAL TIME:** 1 hour 30 minutes

SPICY ITALIAN SAUSAGE MEATLOAF

- **3 slices white sandwich bread, fresh or left out for a day**
- **⅓ cup whole milk**
- **1 cup roughly chopped mushrooms**
- **1 pound hot Italian sausage (bulk, or casings removed)**
- **1 pound ground beef**
- **1 cup finely chopped onions**
- **1 cup finely grated carrots**
- **1 large egg**
- **1 tablespoon Worcestershire sauce**
- **2 teaspoons kosher salt**
- **1 teaspoon red pepper flakes**
- **½ teaspoon freshly ground black pepper**
- **¼ cup ketchup**
- **2 tablespoons brown sugar**

Man, I love meatloaf. And not just for the nostalgia of it. Truth is, we didn't make it a ton growing up. But I DID love it in those frozen TV dinners. I even loved it covered in that horrific-looking gel they called sauce.

Now, of course, I prefer my meatloaf made of actual, you know, meat. And not just any meat, the gift that is spicy Italian sausage. If your fingers aren't, at some point, slopping up the saucy sides of the pan, you have some serious restraint.

Preheat the oven to 350°F.

In a food processor, process the bread to fine crumbs (1 cup). Transfer the bread crumbs to a large bowl, cover them with the milk, and let soak for 5 minutes.

In the processor, mince the mushrooms until fine. Add to the bread crumbs along with the sausage, beef, onions, carrots, egg, Worcestershire sauce, salt, red pepper flakes, and black pepper. Gently mix with your hands, until just combined. (If you mash it up too much, the meatloaf gets tough. A tough meatloaf gets no love.)

Coat a 9 × 5-inch loaf pan with cooking spray or grease it with butter and place the meatloaf mixture in the pan. In a small bowl, stir together the ketchup and brown sugar and coat the top of the meatloaf with it.

Bake until the meatloaf is cooked through and the glaze is slightly dried, about 1 hour. Let cool slightly before slicing. Some liquid will pool in the bottom of the pan. Some will be absorbed back into the meatloaf as it cools; sop up the rest with bread!

SERVES 6

PREP TIME: 20 minutes **TOTAL TIME:** 45 minutes

SPICY CAJUN SAUSAGE, PEPPERS, AND CABBAGE

- **1½ pounds green cabbage, cut into 2-inch-wide wedges**
- **¼ cup plus 2 tablespoons extra-virgin olive oil**
- **Kosher salt**
- **½ teaspoon freshly ground black pepper**
- **1½ pounds andouille sausage, cut into ¼-inch-thick slices**
- **1 large onion, sliced into half-moons**
- **2 large green bell peppers, sliced**
- **1 red bell pepper, sliced**
- **1½ teaspoons Cajun seasoning, store-bought or homemade (page 35)**
- **3 tablespoons roughly chopped garlic**
- **¾ cup low-sodium chicken broth or water**

I remember approximately two hours of my last trip to New Orleans. Much of it was spent drinking those horrific alcoholic slushies—that's the part I do not remember. So the trip was basically ten hours of sleep and two hours of coming back to life through the magic of a plate of sausage and peppers. I feel like an idiot even trying to tell you how good cabbage is nestled into a skillet of Cajun-seasoned andouille sausage and sweet peppers. And when those elements get that nice, salty almost-black char on the bottom? You've made it, kid.

In a bowl, toss the cabbage with 2 tablespoons of the olive oil, ½ teaspoon salt, and the pepper and set aside.

In the biggest skillet you have (at least 12 inches), heat the remaining ¼ cup oil over medium-high heat. Add the andouille and cook, stirring occasionally, until browned, about 5 minutes. Add the onion, bell peppers, and Cajun seasoning and cook, stirring, until the onions soften and brown, 8 to 10 minutes. Stir in the garlic and cook for 2 minutes more.

Nestle the cabbage in under the sausage and peppers (move all the sausage stuff to one side of the pan, drop in some cabbage, smother it back with the sausage and add the cabbage to the other side. The point is you want the cabbage to be touching the hot surface of the pan). Add the broth, reduce the heat to medium-low, cover tightly with foil or a lid, and cook until the underside of the cabbage is browned, about 15 minutes. Uncover, flip the cabbage, and cook until the cabbage is tender, about 10 minutes longer. Season to taste with salt and serve.

SERVES 4 TO 6

PREP TIME: 25 minutes **TOTAL TIME:** 4 hours 30 minutes

JOHN'S MARINATED STEAKS

for the **MARINADE**

- ½ cup soy sauce
- ½ cup extra-virgin olive oil
- Finely grated zest of 1 lemon
- 6 tablespoons fresh lemon juice
- ⅓ cup Worcestershire sauce
- ¼ cup finely chopped fresh basil
- 2 tablespoons finely minced garlic
- 2 tablespoons dried parsley or chopped fresh parsley
- 1 tablespoon Dijon mustard
- 2 teaspoons red pepper flakes
- 1 teaspoon ground white pepper
- 1 teaspoon freshly ground black pepper
- 1 teaspoon kosher salt
- 1 teaspoon sugar
- 1 teaspoon dried minced garlic

- 4 (1-pound) bone-in rib-eye steaks

I'm not one to brag, but luckily, John exists! And he doesn't mind calling this marinade "perfect." And he couldn't be more right because this makes me actually admit I'm wrong in thinking the perfect way to make steak is simply salt, pepper, and a grill.

I would probably still go simple if I was staring at the most beautiful piece of beef I've ever seen, but use this tangy marinade on a nice, solid rib eye and I promise you, it'll be hard for you to have it any other way.

MAKE THE MARINADE: In a dish large enough to hold the steaks, combine all of the marinade ingredients.

Place the steaks in the marinade, turn to coat, and refrigerate for at least 4 hours and up to 24 hours.

Remove the steaks from the marinade and pat them dry with paper towels. (If you want to make a quickie steak sauce, reserve the marinade and see below.)

Heat a grill or grill pan over medium-high heat until smoking hot. Add the steaks and grill without moving for 2 minutes, then turn them 90 degrees to get those fancy hatch marks. Cook for another 2 to 3 minutes, until the steak is really nicely browned, and flip. Cook 4 minutes longer for medium-rare, or to your preferred doneness.

Remove from the grill and let rest on a platter for 4 minutes. (You can cover with foil to keep warm). Serve.

quickie steak sauce

Cut 4 tablespoons (½ stick) cold butter into chunks. Transfer the reserved marinade to a small saucepan and bring to a boil over medium heat, then lower the heat to a gentle simmer. Whisk in the butter, a chunk or two at a time, until glossy and delicious. Remove from the heat and season to taste with salt and pepper. Serve with the steaks.

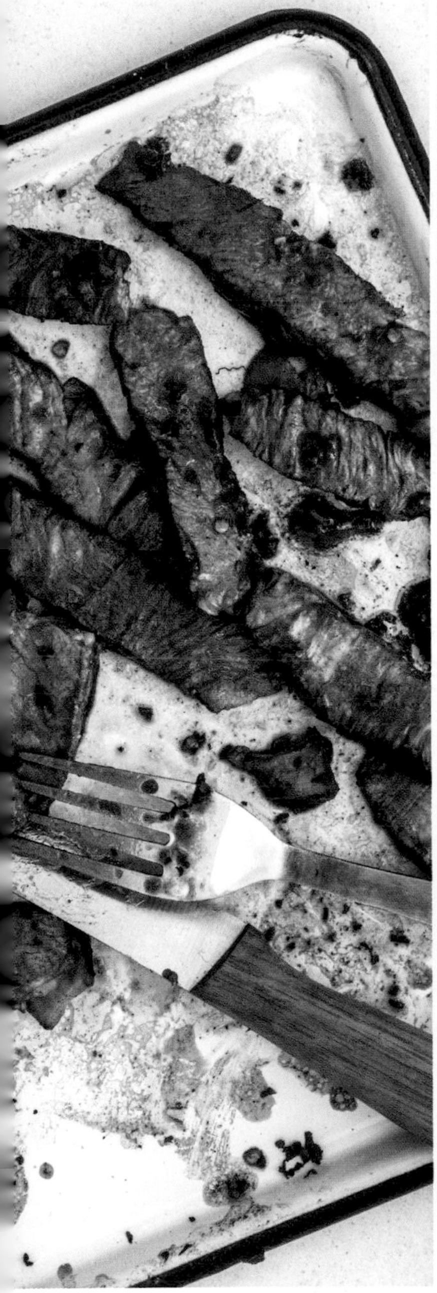

SERVES 4 TO 6

TOTAL TIME: 30 minutes

SKILLET-CHARRED FISH TACOS

When I had to move and leave behind everyone in Washington, just before senior year at Snohomish High School, and start allllllllllll over in Huntington Beach, California, I seriously thought life was over, like OHHHH MY GOD THERE IS NO WAY YOU ARE DOING THIS TO ME DAD like everything I have is here seriously these are going to be my friends for life and we are gonna run around corn mazes forever and ever and I am gonna marry [name redacted] LIKE OHHHHH MY GOD HOW COULD YOU?

You are gonna think I am bullshitting you with the shittiest of bulls here but there is ONE thing and one thing only that stopped me from crying after my first day as a Huntington High Oiler: the fish tacos at Wahoo's.

Wahoo's Fish Tacos was not something we Snohos (Other schools called us this. Excuse me, I am a strong and powerful, sexually aware human female, thank you.) were exactly familiar with. After that first day of school, I ventured down to HB Main Street to job hunt and passed by the sticker-adorned walls of this fine establishment. I ordered a grilled fish taco, and life was forever changed. I ate a fish taco EVERY SINGLE DAY after my shift at Huntington Surf and Sport.

POINT, YOU ASK? My first fish taco stopped my tears. This fish taco brings me to them. Using my mom's hot green pepper sauce instead of salsa might bring tears to your eyes, too.

for the **SPICY MAYO**

- ½ cup mayonnaise
- ¼ cup Sriracha

for the **FISH**

- 3 tablespoons chili powder
- 1½ tablespoons minced garlic (about 2 cloves)
- 1½ teaspoons kosher salt
- ½ teaspoon freshly ground black pepper
- 3 tablespoons canola oil
- 1½ pounds tilapia fillets (or your favorite white fish)

for the **TACOS**

- 12 corn tortillas
- 1 cup finely shredded red cabbage
- 2 small tomatoes, diced
- 6 radishes, thinly sliced or julienned
- ½ cup sliced scallions
- 1 large avocado, sliced
- Pepper's Hot Green Pepper Sauce (page 113), for serving
- Cilantro sprigs and lime wedges, for serving

MAKE THE SPICY MAYO: In a bowl, stir together the mayo and Sriracha until smooth.

COOK THE FISH: In a bowl, combine the chili powder, garlic, salt, pepper, and 1½ tablespoons of the oil. Rub the spice mixture all over the fish. Heat a cast-iron skillet over medium-high heat. Add the remaining 1½ tablespoons oil and when the oil just starts to smoke, add the fish in one layer and cook until slightly charred, 3 minutes per side. Remove from the heat, cool, and flake the fish.

ASSEMBLE THE TACOS: Warm the tortillas, two by two, in a dry skillet set over medium heat, flipping after a few seconds. Stack the hot tortillas to keep them warm.

Spread 1 tablespoon of the spicy mayo on each tortilla, then top with some fish. Top each taco with some cabbage, tomato, radish, and scallion. Then top each taco with avocado. Drizzle with some of Pepper's hot green pepper sauce. Garnish with cilantro and serve with lime wedges.

MAKES 4 SANDWICHES

TOTAL TIME: 40 minutes

DAD'S FRIED FISH SANDWICH

WITH COLESLAW AND TARTAR SAUCE

for the **COLESLAW**

- 1 cup shredded red cabbage
- 1 cup shredded green cabbage
- 1 tablespoon vegetable oil
- 1 tablespoon distilled white vinegar
- ¼ teaspoon kosher salt
- ¼ teaspoon freshly ground black pepper

for the **TARTAR SAUCE**

- 1 cup mayonnaise
- 5 tablespoons finely chopped yellow onion
- ¼ cup finely chopped sweet pickles
- 2 tablespoons finely chopped dill pickles
- 2 cloves garlic, minced or grated
- Kosher salt and freshly ground black pepper

for the **SANDWICHES**

- 8 King's Hawaiian slider buns
- Softened unsalted butter, for spreading on the buns
- 4 slices American cheese, quartered

We all know about Mama Pepper, perhaps too much. But what do we really know about the enigma that is Ron Teigen?

Everyone thinks Mom and I are so alike. But would you dare believe that I am actually more like Pops, aside from our tastes in fishing vests? Mom and I share our spunk and energy but Dad and I are *sensitivos,* fragile like a delicate chocolate soufflé.

Before the blessing that is me, Mom and Dad owned a tavern, named Porky's, which is actually where Pepper became Pepper, thanks to her love of spice and a few not-so-creative drunks.

Also bred out of the tavern was my dad's tartar sauce. Years before, Dad went on a lifelong mission to copy the tartar sauce he dubbed the most epic sauce to ever adorn his mouth, a sauce from a place called Cap'n Yobi's. In a painter's bucket in the back of Porky's, that mission was fulfilled.

So slather that sweet tartar sauce onto this crispy fish sammie with tangy slaw, and you'll be eating an old piece of Teigen history.

MAKE THE COLESLAW: In a large bowl, combine the cabbages, oil, vinegar, salt, and pepper.

MAKE THE TARTAR SAUCE: In a small bowl, combine the mayo, onion, pickles, and garlic. Season to taste with salt and pepper.

// *recipe continues*

Dad's Fried Fish Sandwiches with Zucchini Fries (PAGE 172)

for the
FISH AND BATTER

- **Vegetable oil, for frying**
- **¾ cup cold seltzer water**
- **¼ cup really cold vodka (from a frozen bottle if possible)**
- **1 large egg, beaten**
- **¾ cup all-purpose flour**
- **⅓ cup cornstarch**
- **Kosher salt and freshly ground black pepper**
- **1 pound thin halibut fillets, cut into 8 (2 × 1-inch) rectangles**

PREP THE BUNS: Preheat the oven to 450°F.

Set up the buns by halving and arranging them cut side up on a baking sheet. Butter them to taste and put some cheese on each top bun. Set aside while you cook the fish.

BATTER AND FRY THE FISH: Heat 4 inches of oil in a big pot over medium-high heat until it reaches 375°F on a deep-fry thermometer (get one!) or until a few drops of batter sizzle immediately on contact.

In a big bowl, whisk together the seltzer, vodka, and egg—gently, so you don't unfizz the seltzer. In a medium bowl, combine the flour, cornstarch, and 1½ teaspoons salt. Add the flour mixture to the wet ingredients and stir until they're just combined (there may be a few small lumps, which is totally fine).

When the oil is ready, dip the fish into the batter 3 or 4 pieces at a time and carefully lower the pieces into the hot oil. (Use tongs if you'd like, but whatever you do don't drop them in and splash yourself with hot oil!) Fry until golden brown and crisp, 2 to 3 minutes per batch, then drain the fish on paper towels. Season them with a little salt and pepper while they're still hot.

ASSEMBLE THE SANDWICHES: Warm the buns in the oven until the cheese just begins to melt and the edges are toasty, 2 to 3 minutes. Spread some tartar sauce on each bottom bun, then pile on a little coleslaw. Place a piece of fried fish on top of the coleslaw and close each sandwich with a bun top. Serve right away.

SERVES 4 TO 8

PREP TIME: 35 minutes **TOTAL TIME:** 3 hours 15 minutes

CHIPOTLE-HONEY CHICKEN WITH MANGO-AVOCADO SALSA

for the **CHIPOTLE SAUCE (MAKES 2½ CUPS; SEE NOTE, PAGE 214)**

- 1½ (7-ounce) cans chipotle chiles in adobo
- 1½ cups your favorite barbecue sauce
- ½ cup (packed) light brown sugar
- ¼ cup bourbon or whiskey
- 20 cloves garlic
- Juice of 1 lime

for the **CHICKEN**

- 4 large bone-in, skin-on chicken thighs
- 4 bone-in, skin-on chicken drumsticks
- Kosher salt and freshly ground black pepper
- 3 to 4 tablespoons honey

for the **MANGO SALSA**

- 1 large, firm mango, pitted and finely diced (see page 214)
- ½ firm avocado, diced
- 3 tablespoons finely diced red onion
- ¼ cup (loosely packed) cilantro leaves
- Grated zest and juice of ½ lime, or more to taste
- Kosher salt and freshly ground black pepper

This chicken is my pride and joy. My first born. My identical twin.

The very first recipe to ever hit my blog, no other dish has evolved quite like this one. It started off with a hodgepodge of canned chipotles, a scoop of brown sugar, maybe some lime, a lumberjack's handful of garlic, and some vodka because why not. Measuring wasn't my strong suit in those days.

After countless comments simultaneously praising its flavor and dumping on how it . . . makes you . . . well, it was spicy . . . I decided to veer it more into socially acceptable spicy BBQ territory. But that was boring. Sure, it was tasty. Spicy. Tender. Sweet. But we aren't here just for good food!! We are here for food that'll make your taste buds jump! Food that makes people beg you for the recipe, but you deliberately leave one ingredient off, because that's *your* recipe, mmmkay?

This is that delicious, sweet, sweet baby of mine, perfected. And I didn't even leave any ingredients out. Love you.

MAKE THE CHIPOTLE SAUCE: In a blender or food processor, combine the chipotles, barbecue sauce, brown sugar, bourbon, garlic, and lime juice and process until smooth, about 30 seconds.

MAKE THE CHAACKEN: Season the chicken generously with salt and pepper and place the pieces in a glass baking dish or large zip-top bag. Add 2 cups of the chipotle sauce to coat the chicken. Refrigerate for at least 2 hours and up to 1 day.

// *recipe continues*

Preheat the oven to 375°F. Line a baking sheet with foil.

Remove the chicken from the marinade (the chicken should still be nicely covered in it) and transfer to the baking sheet. Arrange the chicken in one layer. Bake until almost cooked through and the edges are beginning to be charred and crusty, about 35 minutes.

Remove the chicken from the oven, brush with the remaining ½ cup chipotle sauce, drizzle with the honey, and return to the oven and bake until cooked through, about 10 minutes longer.

MEANWHILE, MAKE THE MANGO SALSA: In a bowl, toss together the mango, avocado, onion, cilantro, lime zest, lime juice, and salt and pepper to taste.

Serve the chicken with the salsa.

note

If you want, you can double the sauce and freeze half of it in a zip-top plastic bag so you can have some ready whenever you want it. (The alcohol keeps it scoopable even when frozen.) It's also great sauteed with shrimp.

cutting a mango

To pit a mango, use a peeler to peel the mango, then turn it on its narrow side. Use a sharp knife and make a cut in the mango about ½ inch from where you think the center is. Press down, trying to cut as close to the pit as possible. Repeat with the other side so you have two nice oval-shaped pieces of mango. Dice or cut to your desired shape, and eat the piece with the pit yourself. You deserve it.

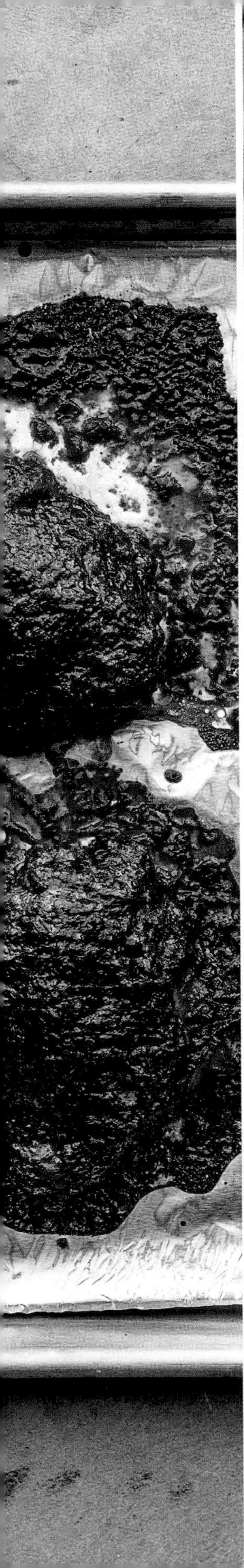

SERVES 4 TO 6

PREP TIME: 40 minutes **TOTAL TIME:** 2 hours 30 minutes

BTI (BETTER THAN INA'S) ROAST CHICKEN AND VEGETABLES

A few years ago, two words changed my entire life. It wasn't "Sports Illustrated" or "prenuptial agreement" but: COMPOUND BUTTER.

Previously, when pure joy was merely a feeling I thought I knew, I lived in a world where I had never once thought about mixing delicious things into delicious butter. Those days are gone now, and I find myself rarely using butter that hasn't been erotically massaged with miso, garlic, toasted sesame oil, herbs, or hot sauce.

Few things are more beautiful than a giant, deep golden brown featherless bird in the middle of a dinner table (unless that bird is turkey, which we can all surely agree sucks and yet once a year we all come together and lie to ourselves and each other for some wild reason). And to go along with such beauty, I think you'll find stuffing chunks of herb butter under the skin and shoving lemons and garlic up the bum to be quite therapeutic. Some people pay for that kind of thing.

- 1 large (5- to 6-pound) roasting chicken (go big or go home)
- Kosher salt and freshly ground black pepper
- 1 stick (4 ounces) unsalted butter, at room temperature
- 23 cloves garlic (8 minced, 15 whole)
- 3 tablespoons mixed chopped herbs (rosemary, thyme, oregano), plus some whole herb sprigs
- 1 lemon
- 4 medium carrots, peeled and cut into large chunks
- 3 parsnips, peeled and cut into large chunks
- 1 onion, cut into 1-inch wedges

Preheat the oven to 350°F.

Remove the bag from the center of the chicken that contains all of the innards and give it to an Asian Mom if you have one—it's like the prize in the Cracker Jack box! Pat the chicken really dry with paper towels, then season it generously both on the inside and the outside with 2 teaspoons salt and ½ teaspoon pepper.

In a bowl, combine the butter, minced garlic, chopped herbs, and a few pinches each of salt and pepper. Grate the lemon's zest right into the bowl, then stir everything together.

Insert your fingers between the chicken skin and the breast to loosen the skin around the meat. It feels kinda dirty, but you'll like it. Slip half the butter mixture underneath the skin, trying really hard not to rip the skin. Halve the zested lemon and stuff the halves inside the chicken's cavity along with 5 of the whole garlic cloves and the herb sprigs. Slather the chicken with the rest of the herb butter.

note

Don't use a large roasting pan unless you're nestling a couple of chickens in there—the drippings will disperse too thinly and evaporate, leaving you with (1) no gravy and (2) dry, sad chicken (a.k.a. turkey).

Arrange the carrots, parsnips, onion, and remaining 10 whole garlic cloves in a 9 × 13-inch baking dish (see Note) in a single layer. Season the vegetables with a few pinches of salt and place the chicken on top, breast-side down. Roast the chicken until it's super golden and the skin is crisp, 1 hour 30 minutes to 1 hour 45 minutes, basting with the juices in the pan every 15 minutes. (This way the skin on the chicken's back will be golden and the skin on the breasts will remain soft, but the breast meat will stay super juicy. If you want golden skin all around, carefully flip the chicken for the last 30 minutes of roasting.)

Remove from the oven, let cool for 10 minutes, then transfer the chicken to a cutting board. Drain the cooking juices into a container, and use a gravy baster thingie to suck off and discard the butter floating on top (or save it for another use). Remove the lemon halves from the chicken and squeeze one or both of them into the juices and season to taste with salt and pepper. Remove the other stuff from inside the chicken and discard. Carve the chicken and serve it with the vegetables and the chicken juices.

SERVES 4

PREP TIME: 30 minutes **TOTAL TIME:** 2 hours 30 minutes

JOHN'S TUSCAN BRICK CHICKEN WITH CHARRED LEMONS

Brick chicken is so heavily demanded by our loved ones that it drives me to the point of insanity. Good thing it's damn easy.

The first time I made it, the biggest difficulty was actually getting the bricks. I mean have you seen the parking lot at Home Depot????? It's like freaking Grand Theft Auto meets Mario Kart. I've never seen so much pure chaos. And let me tell you, they are really weirded out by you buying exactly two bricks.

But once you have said bricks?? Your entire chicken-cooking world changes. The bricks weight the chicken down, pressing its skin against the pan and making sure it all crisps up, and the meat inside is locked up like the Fort Knox of chicken juiciness. And then you'll be in the same boat as me. Having to make this herby bird every goddamned weekend.

⅓ cup extra-virgin olive oil

3 tablespoons chopped fresh rosemary

3 tablespoons chopped fresh sage

2 tablespoons very finely minced garlic (about 4 cloves)

1½ teaspoons red pepper flakes

Kosher salt

1½ teaspoons freshly ground black pepper

Grated zest of 2 lemons, plus 2 skin-on lemons, quartered

4 bone-in, skin-on chicken leg quarters

2 tablespoons canola oil

special **EQUIPMENT**

2 bricks (they're like a dollar at Home Depot!)

In a bowl, combine the olive oil, rosemary, sage, garlic, red pepper flakes, 1½ teaspoons salt, the pepper, and lemon zest. Pat the chicken dry and place it in a baking dish. Rub the herb mixture all over the chicken, cover, and refrigerate for at least 2 hours and up to 24 hours.

Double-wrap the bricks in heavy duty foil (this is your workout for the day). Heat a large cast-iron skillet over medium-high heat until hot. Add the canola oil, then add the chicken, skin-side down, and weight it down with the bricks. (If they don't all fit comfortably, use 2 pans, or cook in batches.) Cook, without moving the chicken, for 7 to 9 minutes, or until the underside is crisped and mahogany brown (don't lift it, which means be a more patient person than me). Remove the bricks, flip the chicken, weight it down with the bricks again, and continue to cook until the underside is browned and the meat is cooked through, 7 to 9 minutes. (If the skin on the first side seemed too dark, reduce the heat to medium. To check if the meat is done, pierce the thickest part with a knife; if the juices that come out have no pink, it's done.)

Remove the chicken from the pan, add the quartered lemons, and sear until slightly charred and caramelized, about 2 minutes per side. Serve the chicken with more salt to taste and the charred lemons for squeezing.

SERVES 4 TO 6

PREP TIME: 45 minutes **TOTAL TIME:** 4 hours 45 minutes

MARGARITA CHICKEN FAJITAS
WITH MUSHROOMS AND SPINACH

for the **CHICKEN**

- ¼ cup olive oil
- Grated zest of 1 lime
- ¼ cup fresh lime juice
- ¼ cup tequila
- 3 tablespoons adobo sauce (from a can of chipotles in adobo)
- 2 tablespoons fresh orange juice
- 2 tablespoons minced garlic (about 3 cloves)
- 1 teaspoon sugar
- 2 teaspoons kosher salt
- 1 teaspoon freshly ground black pepper
- 2 pounds boneless, skinless chicken thighs
- 2 tablespoons canola or vegetable oil

Seeing a sizzling hot plate of fajitas make their way down the aisle of a restaurant called Azteca is one of my earliest memories. The eyes of the person who ordered them would always light up, as everyone else's eyes burned from both the smoke and the regret from not ordering fajitas. That sound! That sizzle. That smell of caramelizing onions and peppers. That meat you can just feel is overcooking. I love everything about the damn thing.

So what makes these "margarita" fajitas? The lime. The salt. The tequila. OK, so they're more like body-shot fajitas, but just roll with me here. Wait, there is orange juice! Is that in a margarita? I'm usually pretty tanked off margaritas when I make them, so I don't remember.

MAKE THE CHICKEN: In a big bowl, combine the olive oil, lime zest, lime juice, tequila, adobo sauce, orange juice, garlic, sugar, salt, and pepper. Add the chicken, toss to coat, and refrigerate for at least 4 hours and up to 24 hours.

Preheat the oven to 200°F.

Lift the chicken out of the marinade, wipe off any excess, and keep 1 cup of the marinade. In an extra-large heavy skillet, heat the oil over medium-high heat until shimmering-hot. Sear the chicken, working in batches if it doesn't all fit comfortably, until the underside is browned, about 5 minutes. Flip the chicken and cook until the other side is browned, about 5 minutes longer. Cut into the chicken; if there's any pink left inside, turn the heat down to medium and cook for another few minutes to finish. Remove from the heat, transfer to an ovenproof bowl, cover with foil, and keep warm in the oven. Do not clean the skillet.

// *recipe continues*

for the
FAJITAS

- **1 tablespoon canola or vegetable oil**
- **1 large red onion, sliced**
- **1 tablespoon chopped garlic**
- **3 cups sliced mushrooms**
- **4 cups (packed) baby spinach**
- **Kosher salt and freshly ground black pepper**
- **8 medium (6-inch) flour tortillas**
- **2 cups shredded pepper jack cheese**
- **Sliced fresh or pickled jalapeño peppers, for garnish**
- **Chopped tomatoes, for garnish**

MAKE THE FAJITAS: Heat the oil in the same skillet you used to cook the chicken over medium heat. Add the red onion and stir to scrape up the browned chicken bits. Cook the onion, stirring occasionally, until well browned, 10 to 12 minutes. Add the garlic and cook for 1 minute. Add the mushrooms and cook until they release their liquid, 6 to 7 minutes. Add the spinach and cook until wilted, 1 to 2 minutes. Season to taste with salt and pepper, transfer to a bowl, and cover with foil to keep warm. Add the reserved marinade to the skillet and bring to a boil.

Remove the chicken from the oven and shred into bite-size pieces; taste one and season with more salt if necessary.

Set a dry skillet over medium-high heat and warm the tortillas in it, one by one, about 15 seconds per side. Stack the tortillas to keep them warm.

Set the tortillas out with the bowls of chicken and onion mixture. Drizzle some of the boiled marinade on the chicken to keep it moist. Set out more bowls with the pepper jack cheese, jalapeños, and tomatoes and let people build their own fajitas.

MAKES 4 SANDWICHES

PREP TIME: 25 minutes **TOTAL TIME:** 40 minutes

"EVERYTHING" CHICKEN SANDWICH MELTS

for the **CHICKEN**

- 2 tablespoons extra-virgin olive oil
- 2 teaspoons paprika
- 1 teaspoon cayenne pepper
- 1 teaspoon kosher salt
- 1 teaspoon freshly ground black pepper
- 4 thin-cut chicken breast cutlets (5 ounces each)

for the **BREADING**

- ½ cup all-purpose flour
- 1 tablespoon paprika
- 1 teaspoon kosher salt
- ½ teaspoon freshly ground black pepper
- 1 tablespoon cayenne pepper
- 2 eggs
- 1½ cups plain dried bread crumbs
- 3 tablespoons sesame seeds
- 3 tablespoons dried minced onion flakes
- 2 tablespoons dried minced garlic
- 1 tablespoon poppy seeds
- 1½ teaspoons caraway seeds

OK, I know that half of the recipes in this book feel like they were either developed BY people with a bogus medical marijuana card, or FOR them. But like many decisions made under one influence or another, this one has its own crazy genius. Everything bagels are, indeed, *everything*, so I took allllll those delicious seeds and flavors and decided to bread and pan-fry a juicy chicken bust into a salty, oniony, garlicky, crispy little cutlet. Slap that onto some flatbread, add cheese, possibly even a tomato and a red onion slice (because, you know, vegetables) and broil this magic into an open-faced sammie. Seriously, this sandwich is crazy delicious, and if you don't want the sandwich you can make the cutlet and cut it up over salad. (File under: Sober Stoner Recipes.)

PREPARE THE CHICKEN: In a small bowl, combine the olive oil, paprika, cayenne, salt, and black pepper. Rub the mixture all over the chicken.

SET UP THE BREADING STATION: In a wide, shallow bowl, combine the flour, paprika, salt, black pepper, and cayenne. In a second wide, shallow bowl, beat the eggs just to combine. In a third wide, shallow dish, combine the bread crumbs, sesame seeds, onion flakes, dried garlic, poppy seeds, and caraway seeds.

Working with one cutlet at a time, place the chicken in the flour to coat, shake off the excess, dip both sides in the egg, shaking off any excess, then press into the bread crumb mixture, shaking off any excess. Transfer the breaded chicken cutlets to a plate.

// recipe continues

for the **SANDWICH MELTS**

- Canola oil, for shallow-frying
- 4 (8-inch) round soft lavash or naan breads
- 2 tablespoons extra-virgin olive oil
- 1 cup shredded cheddar cheese
- ½ large red onion, sliced into ¼-inch-thick rings
- 1 large beefsteak tomato, cut into 8 (¼-inch-thick) slices
- Kosher salt and freshly ground black pepper
- 8 slices pepper jack cheese

MAKE THE SANDWICH MELTS: Position a rack 6 inches from the heating element and preheat the broiler.

In a large skillet, heat ¼ inch canola oil over medium-high heat until shimmering-hot. Working in two to three batches, add the cutlets and fry until golden and crisp, 2 to 3 minutes per side, adding a little more oil if needed between batches. Drain the cutlets on paper towels.

Trim the bread to about the size of the chicken cutlets or a little larger. Arrange on a baking sheet, brush with the olive oil, and sprinkle ¼ cup cheddar evenly over each lavash. Divide the onion rings among the lavash, then top each with a fried cutlet. Arrange 2 tomato slices on top of each cutlet, season with salt and pepper, and layer pepper jack cheese on top of each cutlet.

Broil the sandwiches until the cheese is bubbling and slightly browned, 3 to 4 minutes. Serve hot.

CHEESY JALAPEÑO TUNA CASSEROLE WITH POTATO CHIP TOPPING

SERVES 8 TO 10

PREP TIME: 20 minutes **TOTAL TIME:** 1 hour 15 minutes

True story: So I was trying to only drink juice for a few days before shooting the f*cking *Sports Illustrated Swimsuit* issue, only my most important job every year and the one that basically made my career. But then at the photo shoot for this cookbook you are reading, some genius thought it would be a good idea to surround me with bags upon bags of Tim's Cascade Jalapeño chips. They own me. I mean, they're so crunchy that when I was a kid I couldn't even sneak them in class—I'd just lick the seasoning off to satisfy my addiction until the bell. Sure enough, within 30 seconds I was so deep into that bag I basically needed to be fished out with a net.

This tuna casserole is made with cans, cans, cans, and that's the way I like it, thank you very much. (Make sure to get the chunk solid tuna or it kind of breaks up all over the noodles. Can you tell I've been hurt before?) Of course, because I love everything in moderation, I added way more cheese than normal, more canned soup to make it really creamy, threw in fresh chopped jalapeño peppers, then piled the entire thing with Tim's Cascade Jalapeño chips. And now Tim's Cascade chips will own you, too.

for the **CASSEROLE**

- Kosher salt
- 1 pound corkscrew pasta
- 3 (10.75-ounce) cans condensed cream of mushroom soup
- 3 (5-ounce) cans water-packed tuna, drained
- 1½ cups whole milk
- 1 cup frozen peas, thawed
- ⅓ cup chopped celery
- ¼ cup finely chopped fresh jalapeño peppers (leave the seeds in if you're a glutton for punishment)
- 3 cups shredded extra-sharp cheddar cheese
- 1 teaspoon freshly ground black pepper

for the **TOPPING**

- 3 cups jalapeño-flavor potato chips (preferably Tim's Cascade brand), crushed
- 1½ cups shredded extra-sharp cheddar cheese

PREPARE THE CASSEROLE: Preheat the oven to 350°F. Coat a deep 9 × 13-inch baking dish with cooking spray or grease it with butter.

In a large pot of salted boiling water, cook the pasta 2 minutes less than the package directions, so they're a little underdone. Drain.

In a large bowl, combine the drained pasta, mushroom soup, tuna, milk, peas, celery, jalapeños, cheddar, 2 teaspoons salt, and the black pepper. Pour into the baking dish.

MAKE THE TOPPING: In a bowl, combine the potato chips and cheddar. Scatter the mixture on top of the casserole.

Bake until bubbling and the topping is golden brown, 50 to 55 minutes.

SERVES 2

PREP TIME: 10 minutes **TOTAL TIME:** 25 minutes

SUPER TUNA MELTS

- **2 (5-ounce) cans water-packed white tuna, drained**
- **½ cup mayonnaise**
- **⅓ cup finely diced onion**
- **2 tablespoons sweet pickle relish**
- **1 tablespoon Dijon mustard**
- **Kosher salt and freshly ground black pepper**
- **4 tablespoons (½ stick) unsalted butter, at room temperature**
- **4 slices country white bread**
- **6 slices vine-ripened tomato**
- **6 thick or 12 thin cheddar cheese slices**

I love tuna in all forms so much that one of those weird, L.A. guru doctor-to-the-stars actually told me he was surprised I was still alive with all the mercury in my system. He came to this conclusion via feeling my abdomen for about 8 seconds as he stared at a Zen garden outside, then sending out for an overpriced blood test. He demanded I never eat tuna again but LUCKILY he had the cure for my toxic poisoning in the form of pills he sold in his office. I mean, how #blessed am I!!

I bought the stupid gut regimen and saw my New York doctor for a second opinion. He ran an actual doctor-who-went-to-a-school-with-grades blood test and not only were my mercury levels not sky-high, they were zero.

Lesson learned. I should have known not to go to a doctor who looked like a mix of one of those Burning Man sweat lodge lords and some sort of Tantric sex healer. I don't even know what that means, but just piece it together and picture it, OK!?

Oh, ummm tuna. I know my tuna, therefore I make the best effing tuna sandwich. I butter the bread to within an inch of its life and then fry the whole thing in a skillet until the cheddar melts into a cheesy river and the bread is basically a giant buttery cracker. After eating this sandwich I always decide that mercury poisoning is worth it and I commit myself to living the rest of my days as a human thermometer.

In a bowl, combine the tuna, mayo, onion, relish, mustard, ½ teaspoon salt, and ¼ teaspoon pepper and mix until incorporated.

Spread 1 tablespoon of butter on one side of each piece of bread, then flip the slices over so they are buttered-side down. Divide the tuna mixture between 2 slices of bread, then top with the tomato slices and cheddar. Place the remaining 2 slices of bread on top, buttered-side up.

Heat a heavy skillet over low heat and toast the sandwiches in it until the cheese is melted and the bread is golden and toasty, 5 to 6 minutes per side.

SERVES 4

PREP TIME: 10 minutes **TOTAL TIME:** 2 hours 30 minutes

LITERALLY STOVETOP PORK CHOPS

There is a running joke in my life that I am chock-full of ideas, but have no sense of how to actually execute them. I'll say an idea, I'll whisper it into the palm of my hand, then blow it into thin air so maybe, just maybe, someone else will make it happen. Pulverizing Stove Top stuffing and breading pork chops with the herby bread crumbs was an idea I could simply not blow into thin air. And we are all rewarded for it. You're welcome.

for the **BRINE AND PORK**

- ¼ cup kosher salt
- ¼ cup sugar
- 2 teaspoons dried sage
- 2 teaspoons red pepper flakes
- 1 teaspoon cracked black peppercorns
- 2½ cups ice
- 4 boneless pork chops (½ inch thick)

for the **BREADING**

- 2 large eggs
- 1 cup all-purpose flour
- ½ teaspoon kosher salt
- ½ teaspoon freshly ground black pepper
- ¼ teaspoon cayenne pepper
- ½ (6-ounce) package Stove Top Stuffing mix (1½ cups)

- ½ cup canola vegetable oil

BRINE THE PORK CHOPS: In a saucepan, combine 1½ cups water, the salt, sugar, sage, red pepper flakes, and peppercorns. Bring to a boil over high heat and boil until the salt and sugar are dissolved. Transfer to a glass baking dish and add the ice; let the ice melt. Add the pork chops to the brine, cover, and refrigerate for 2 hours.

SET UP THE BREADING STATION: In a shallow bowl, beat the eggs. In a second shallow bowl, combine the flour, salt, black pepper, and cayenne. In a food processor, process the stuffing mix until fine crumbs form and place the crumbs in a third bowl.

Remove the chops from the brine and pat them dry with paper towels. Working with one at a time, dip the chops first in the flour, then in the eggs, then in the crumbs, pressing to make the crumbs stick to each side. Let the breaded chops sit on a plate for a few minutes—it helps the breading stick better.

In a 10-inch heavy skillet, heat ¼ cup of the oil over medium-high heat until shimmering-hot. Add 2 of the chops and fry until golden and crispy, 3 to 4 minutes max per side. Remove, drain on paper towels, and repeat with the remaining oil and pork.

// ***Opposite:*** Literally Stovetop Pork Chops with Charred and Garlicky Broccoli (page 173)

SERVES 4

PREP TIME: 35 minutes **TOTAL TIME:** 1 hour 5 minutes

PROSCIUTTO-WRAPPED STUFFED CHICKEN BREASTS

I hate chicken breast, and chicken thighs make me happier than watching drunk chicks in a club bathroom. But, damn this career choice of mine: I can't just be eating chicken fat all day.

What I CAN do is take a perfectly healthy chicken breast and stuff it with creamy cheese and bacon then wrap the thing in classy, thin-sliced pig. Don't ask how this seems healthier to me.

My favorite part about this recipe is that absolutely anybody can do it, and do it well. It came about by my own personal chicken-breast insecurities—I wanted to make something that would never be called dry and dull. The cheese will ooze out into the pan and onto the burst cherry tomatoes, and you won't be able to help yourself. Spoon that juice all over, you dirty thing, you!

for the **GARLIC HERB CHEESE**

- 2 ounces cream cheese, at room temperature
- 2 ounces fresh goat cheese
- 1½ cloves garlic, finely minced
- ½ tablespoon fresh thyme leaves, finely chopped
- ½ tablespoon fresh oregano leaves, finely chopped
- Kosher salt and fresh ground black pepper

for the **CHICKEN**

- 2 slices bacon
- 2 large boneless, skinless chicken breasts (½ pound each)
- Kosher salt and freshly ground black pepper
- 6 slices prosciutto (2 ounces)
- 2 tablespoons olive oil
- 1 cup cherry tomatoes
- Fresh thyme and oregano sprigs (if you have them)

MAKE THE GARLIC HERB CHEESE: In a food processor (or in a bowl, by hand), combine the cream cheese, goat cheese, garlic, thyme, and oregano. Season to taste with salt and pepper. (The garlic will be strong, but will mellow out when you cook it.)

MAKE THE CHICKEN: Preheat the oven to 350°F.

In a medium cast-iron skillet, cook the bacon over medium heat until crispy, about 8 minutes. Transfer the bacon to paper towels to cool. Pour off excess fat from the skillet, leaving enough to coat the pan. Let the skillet cool.

Place one piece of chicken between two sheets of plastic wrap, then use a meat mallet or the bottom of a heavy skillet to pound the chicken into an even ½-inch thickness (it won't be perfect, and if the edges get raggedy you can trim them if you're OCD like me). Season with salt and pepper. Repeat with the remaining piece of chicken.

Spread each breast with half of the herbed cheese. Crumble the bacon over the cheese and roll up each chicken breast, starting from a short side. Wrap each roll in 3 pieces of prosciutto. Brush each roll with the olive oil and season lightly with pepper.

Place the chicken in the cast-iron skillet, seam-side down, then scatter the tomatoes around the chicken. Throw in the herb sprigs (if using) and bake until the chicken is cooked and some edges of the prosciutto are a little crispy, about 30 minutes.

Let the chicken cool for a few minutes, then slice each roll in half and serve that chaacken with the tomatoes and oozy cheesy juices.

ACKNOWLEDGMENTS

A huge six-foot Vermont teddy bear hug to everyone at Clarkson Potter: Aaron Wehner, Doris Cooper, Marysarah Quinn, Laura Palese, and the eternally patient food genius that is Francis Lam for signing on to this adventure and attending my unconventional open house feast-with-a-side-of-book-publishing meeting. I knew you were my home from the second I met you. I would have gone with you for less but my agents stressed not saying that earlier.

My photo team—Aubrie Pick, Courtney Munna, and Bessma Khalaf—for loving food and animals (and maybe food animals) as much as taking beautiful pictures.

The wildly talented Fanny Pan with Elizabeth Normoyle and Cybelle Tondu: Thank you for making every bite look so beautiful, so crispy, and so deliciously gooey. Thanks also to Brett Long for the cover-shoot food styling.

Alistair Turnbull and Jameson Pabes for your brilliant eyes and for hand-picking things that give me serious kitchen envy.

2010 Studios for being so welcoming and letting us turn your studio into what appeared to be a dog hotel slash late-night diner.

Everyone at 3Arts, WME, IMG, 42West, DSMTFL—Mark, Luke, Andy, Ivan, Lisa, Josh, Jason, Meghan, Erin, Britney, Marisa, Nina, and Abel—for being so supportive of my dream to have an excuse to gain weight. You work harder than any humans should. I would not know how to wake up without you all and I'm eternally grateful for you every single day.

Mary, Kristine, Allan, John, and Anita: Thank you for making that glam time so damn enjoyable. You all are the complete package of talent, hilarity, and nurturingness. (Is that a word? That's the word I want to use.)

Christine Shim: Thank you for being the most on-it person ever to exist, for never having mental breakdowns, and for putting up with all my different Chrissy moods. You are a godsend.

Mom, Dad, Tina, and Pasha: Thank you for providing all the food that shaped this wild palate of mine. For all the meals we enjoyed together growing up, taco fires started, potatoes and tartar sauce consumed. Mom for endlessly washing dishes during the recipe-writing process and opening my taste buds to Thai flavors my entire life. Tina, you are probably a better cook than I am—I love that you appreciate and are knowledgeable about every type of cuisine possible, from fast food to Michelin starred—and will try absolutely anything. Dad, for all the road trips and diners and homemade corned beef and cabbage and chilis and stews. Your love of hearty American food has shaped this belly of mine.

To all of our wonderful friends who came over to taste anything I made, even though I made strategic moves to start dinners hours late so you'd be drunk and hungry and willing to consume it all.

To the real chefs in our lives: Josh Capon for your bite-of-heaven burger and enviable energy. Chef Roblé for countless ladies' nights and apartment party times. Eric (and Sandra!) Ripert for our favorite restaurant, Le Bernardin, introducing me to the magic that is City Harvest, and being just as wonderful as everyone has told me for years.

To my everything, Johnny: Thank you for trying and liking absolutely everything in this book, and for always indulging me in every city by taking me on food adventures I could have never imagined before you. For all the love you shower me with, it makes me so happy to make you happy through food, kisses, and the occasional fake interest in football. I love you more than anything on this earth and beyond, unless you have cheated on me by the time this has been printed.

And to my other everything, Adeena Sussman: Thank you for somehow morphing yourself into a taller, smarter, calmer version of myself. After a week of knowing you, our brains somehow became one, both rattling off recipe ideas like sober stoners. Thank you for moving in with me, taking random trips to Iowa, and always wanting the same bold flavors and perfection. Your sodium levels will never be the same.

INDEX

Note: Page references in *italics* indicate photographs.